T0023967

40 HADITH FROM

Sahih al Bukhari

SHAHRUL HUSSAIN
& ZAHED FETTAH

Forty Hadith from Sahih al-Bukhari

First Published in 2023 by
THE ISLAMIC FOUNDATION

Distributed by
KUBE PUBLISHING LTD
Tel +44 (0)1530 249230
E-mail: info@kubepublishing.com
Website: www.kubepublishing.com

Text copyright © Shahrul Hussain & Zahed Fettah 2023. All rights reserved. No part of this publication may be reproduced, stored in a retrieval system, or transmitted in any form or by any means, electronic, mechanical, photocopying, recording or otherwise, without the prior permission of the copyright owner

Author Shahrul Hussain & Zahed Fettah
Editor Umm Marwan Ibrahim
Cover Design Afreen Fazil (Jaryah Studios)
Arabic/English layout & design Nasir Cadir

A Cataloguing-in-Publication Data record for this book is available from the British Library

ISBN 978-0-86037-935-5
eISBN 978-0-86037-904-9

Printed by Elma Basim, Turkey

Dedication

For Sami and Omaymah

Contents

Introduction

All praise is due to Allah, the Lord of the universe, the Most Merciful the Most Kind, the Master of the Day of Judgement. Peace and blessings be upon Muhammad ﷺ, the final Prophet of Allah, and upon his family and Companions.

Hadith is one of the most important institutions in Islam. It contains the teachings of the Prophet Muhammad ﷺ regarding all aspects of Islam. It is indispensable in order to attain the correct understanding of the religion, and without it, guidance is not possible. Therefore, it is essential for all Muslims to make an effort to understand and study Hadith, even if it is at a basic level.

Unfortunately, most of the works of Hadith literature available in English are long, detailed, and viewed as heavy reads by the general masses. As these are religious texts, it can be daunting for beginners to understand the subject. There are mainly two types of books about Hadith in English. While one type deals with the science of Hadith in terms of its historical phenomena as a vital Islamic institution, the other consists of thick volumes of English renditions of Hadith corpuses—both of which can put off beginners from reading and understanding Hadith.

This dilemma gave birth to the 'Forty Ahadith' project, in which we set out to compile a series of forty ahadith from each of the six canonical books of Hadith. The collection aims to educate people who wish to enjoy Hadith literature without delving too deep into its technicalities. The style and language used in these books is non-specialised and thereby accessible to readers of all levels and ages. As such, the collection is also ideal for new Muslims who wish to learn more about Hadith.

In this particular volume, we have selected forty ahadith from *Ṣaḥīḥ al-Bukhārī* in order to give the reader a flavour of the Hadith literature found within the *Ṣaḥīḥ*. There is no particular reason for choosing the ahadith mentioned herein. However, each hadith will reflect a unique theme so as to touch upon various aspects of the Islamic teachings, such as:

- Manners and Etiquettes
- Character of a Muslim
- Exhortations and Admonitions
- Remembrance of Allah
- Knowledge and Action
- Beliefs

When selecting the forty ahadith for each book in the series, we made sure to avoid lengthy and elaborate narrations or those that dealt with complex legal and theological matters. Instead, you will find that the selected ahadith focus on character, spirituality, morals, manners and ethics, and that the accompanying explanations of the ahadith focus on highlighting these aspects.

Within this volume is a simple discussion of the theoretical parameters of praiseworthy characters every Muslim should aspire to achieve, supererogatory virtuous acts of worship, and the moral philosophy (in particular normative ethics) of these ahadith. It is hoped that this will open the doors for readers to enquire more about Hadith as an important source of revelation.

Finally, it is worth pointing out that the reason for compiling forty ahadith is due to the virtuous nature of 'forty' ahadith recorded in many traditions of the Prophet Muhammad ﷺ. It is related that Prophet Muhammad ﷺ said, 'Whoever memorises forty ahadith regarding the matters of religion, Allah will resurrect him on the Day of Judgement from among the group of jurists and scholars' (*Bayhaqī*). Although this hadith is weak in its authenticity, many scholars have strongly supported acting on weak ahadith, which solely speak about virtues of good deeds, for the sake of spirituality. What is of even more benefit is to memorise forty ahadith from *Ṣaḥīḥ al-Bukhārī* which is the most authentic collection of Hadith literature. The short ahadith in this compilation may help facilitate young learners and beginners to memorise the beloved Prophet's sayings, which would be a great achievement.

We would like to conclude by thanking everyone who has made this project possible, especially Br Haris Ahmad from Kube Publishing House for his support; without his help, this project would not have been possible. The people we are most indebted to are the patrons of the Ibn Rushd Centre of Excellence for Islamic Research. This work is dedicated to them and all those who support the advancement of knowledge and research.

Shahrul Hussain & Zahed Fettah
8th April 2019 / 3rd Shaʿbān 1440

Acknowledgments

It would not be possible to accomplish this work without the support of many great people, too many to mention all of them by name. First and foremost, we thank our parents for their love and support. We are most obliged to mention our heartfelt thanks to Abida Akhtar and Sumayah Ali for their invaluable feedback. A very special heartfelt thanks to Rabiya Dawood and Heba Malick for their fastidious editorial work.

The English language or indeed any other language does not afford a word to express our deepest gratitude to Br Rizvan Khalid for his support and help. We would also like to thank Mr Iqbal Ahmed (OBE, DBA) and Prof Dr Sanawar Choudhury for his kind words of encouragement and all our friends, supporters and volunteers for their support and friendship.

"I ask Allah to raise the rank of my parents and bless them in this life and the next, for they have encouraged me on my path of learning and seeking knowledge."

Zahed Fettah

A Brief Biography of Imam al-Bukhārī

Ṣaḥīḥ al-Bukhārī, the greatest and most important Hadith text in Islamic history, is authored by Abū 'Abdullāh Muḥammad ibn Ismā'īl ibn Ibrāhīm ibn al-Mughīrah ibn Bardizbah al-Bukhārī. He was born in 194 AH (810 CE) in Bukhara, in what is today known as West Turkistan.

Imam al-Bukhārī is considered to be among the leading scholars of Hadith who lived in an era in which Hadith scholars were dominant and many. This gave him the opportunity to be a student of some of the greatest scholars of Hadith in the history of Islam, including Imam Aḥmad ibn Ḥanbal, Imam Isḥāq ibn Rāhwayh, Imam 'Alī ibn al-Madīnī, Imam al-Ḥumaydī, and Imam Yaḥyā ibn Ma'īn. Imam al-Bukhārī's great knowledge of Hadith was something that even his own teachers confirmed. Imam Aḥmad ibn Ḥanbal said: 'Khurasan did not produce anybody like Muḥammad ibn Ismā'īl al-Bukhārī.'

Imam al-Bukhārī was exceptionally intelligent and had a memory that was second to none. He began memorising and studying Hadith when he was only around ten years of age. He continued studying until he became known for his vast knowledge of Hadith whilst he was still a teenager. He himself said: 'I memorise a hundred thousand authentic narrations of Hadith and two hundred thousand weak narrations of Hadith.' What also allowed him to excel above others in his time was his constant travels to many parts of the world seeking knowledge and studying with the leading scholars of Hadith in Makkah, Madinah, Syria, Iraq, Egypt, and elsewhere.

He was known for his piety, righteousness, and worship. He would recite the Qur'an constantly and would complete its recitation in Ramadan every single day. Muḥammad ibn Yūsuf al-Firabrī said that Muḥammad ibn Ismā'īl al-Bukhārī said to him: 'I did not place any hadith in my book *al-Ṣaḥīḥ* except that I would first purify myself and pray two rak'āt (units of prayer).'

With around 7,000 narrations of ahadith recorded in his *Ṣaḥīḥ,* Imam al-Bukhārī helped preserve the Sunnah of the Messenger ﷺ. His contributions to the science of Hadith are exceptional, and scholars after him were heavily reliant upon his great efforts. He was incredibly cautious to narrate hadith from those who have knowledge, and not just anybody. He said: 'I would not write ahadith the way they write. If I wrote a hadith from a person, I would ask about his name, his lineage, and from whom he studied Hadith.'

He authored the most authentic compilation of ahadith that has been authored, known today as *Ṣaḥīḥ al-Bukhārī*. All the scholars of Islam have agreed on the lofty status of this book. However, the status that this great book obtained only came after centuries of studying and critiquing it, which made it clear that Imam al-Bukhārī indeed had done an incredible job. Imam al-Nasā'ī, author of the *Sunan al-Nasā'ī*, said: 'Out of all these books, there is none that is better than the book of Muḥammad ibn Ismā'īl al-Bukhārī.'

Imam al-Bukhārī had arranged his chapters according to various topics of knowledge in Islam, and under each heading he would mention some relevant ahadith. This caused it to not only become a book which contained hadith transmissions, but also a book of *fiqh*, *tafsīr* (Qur'anic interpretation), and *sīrah* (Prophetic biography and that of his Companions). *Ṣaḥīḥ al-Bukhārī* became the most relied upon book of Hadith, and many books were later authored by scholars either explaining the compilation or writing about the methodology of Imam al-Bukhārī. Scholars also examined Imam al-Bukhārī's book to verify that he did indeed collect only rigorously authentic ahadith. And it was only after intense scrutiny that Imam al-Bukhārī received endorsement from all the scholars of Hadith about his great masterpiece.

Some of Imam al-Bukhārī's students who transmitted his hadith collection had developed into leading scholars of Hadith, themselves. The most prominent of these students is Imam Muslim ibn al-Ḥajjāj, the author of what we know today as *Ṣaḥīḥ Muslim*. Other such students include Imam Abū 'Īsā al-Tirmidhī, Imam Muḥammad ibn Naṣr al-Marwazī, and Imam Ibn Khuzaymah, the author of what is known today as *Ṣaḥīḥ Ibn Khuzaymah*.

Imam al-Bukhārī passed away on the 1st of Shawwāl, 256 AH in Khartank, near Samarqand. Incredibly, he passed away on the day of Eid al-Fitr, after spending the month of Ramadan in worship and remembrance of Allah.

The Importance of Hadith and its Significance

Allah sent Messengers throughout history with the objective of clarifying the truth to the people and guiding them to Him. Many of these Messengers were also sent with Books containing guidance, such as the final Messenger of Allah, Prophet Muhammad ﷺ. He was sent to teach the Book, the Qur'an, and to be the living example of the teachings of the Qur'an. As Allah states in the Qur'an: *'Allah has surely conferred a favour on the believers when He sent in their midst a Messenger from among themselves who recites to them His verses, purifies them, and teaches them the Book and the Wisdom, while previously they had been in clear misguidance'* (*Āl 'Imrān* 3: 164). Allah also states: *'And we have sent down the Reminder (the Qur'an) to you so that you (O Messenger) may clarify to the people that which has been sent down to them, and so that they may ponder'* (*al-Naḥl* 16: 44).

These verses highlight that the role of the Messenger ﷺ is to clarify and teach the Qur'an. His words and his actions, which form a verbal and practical interpretation of the Qur'an, is the Prophetic Tradition referred to as the 'Sunnah'. Following the Sunnah is necessary because it is the only way to practice the teachings of the final Book of Allah correctly.

Allah has taken it upon Himself to preserve the Qur'an: *'It is certainly We who have revealed the Reminder, and it is certainly We who will preserve it'* (*al-Ḥijr* 15: 9). This preservation is not restricted to the letters and words of the Qur'an but also includes the preservation of its meanings, which is fulfilled through the Prophetic implementation of the Qur'an—the Sunnah.

It is simply not possible to observe the teachings of Islam without following the Sunnah. The purpose of the Qur'an is to teach us the correct belief and acts of worship Allah demands from us in order to prove our servitude to Him. It is not, however, an instruction manual detailing precise rules and methods of worshipping Allah.

Written or verbal instructions are not enough; it requires a teacher to show us the practical way of worshipping Allah. Thus, while the Qur'an outlines the commandments of Allah such as to fast, give zakat, perform hajj and the like, the role of the Prophet ﷺ is to teach us *how* to perform those acts of worship. Therefore, without knowing and following the Sunnah, Muslims will not be able to observe the teachings of the Qur'an.

Compilation of Hadith

Although the Qur'an was collected and written in one place much earlier than the Hadith, the latter was also preserved in similar ways to the former. Ahadith were written down by some Companions at the time of the Messenger ﷺ, but this habit only became widespread a century or so after the his death.

Since the second century after *hijrah*, many scholars wrote down the Hadith of the Prophet ﷺ. Some scholars compiled books of Hadith which discussed the various areas of the teachings of the Prophet ﷺ. Sadly, some of the earliest books of Hadith were lost. However, some survived and were transmitted throughout centuries until our time, including the *Muwaṭṭa'* of Imam Mālik (d. 179 AH), the *Muṣannaf* of 'Abd al-Razzāq (d. 211 AH), the *Muṣannaf* of Ibn Abī Shaybah (d. 235 AH), and the *Musnad* of Imam Aḥmad ibn Ḥanbal (d. 241 AH). These books contain thousands of reports from the Prophet ﷺ and his Companions, clarifying how they implemented the Qur'anic teachings in their everyday life.

Hundreds of books of Hadith were authored, but only a dozen of them became famous and spread worldwide. The nine most relied-upon books of Hadith are:

1. *Ṣaḥīḥ al-Bukhārī*
2. *Ṣaḥīḥ Muslim*
3. *Sunan Abū Dāwūd*
4. *Sunan al-Tirmidhī*
5. *Sunan al-Nasā'ī*
6. *Sunan Ibn Mājah*
7. *Muwaṭṭa' Mālik*
8. *Musnad Aḥmad*
9. *Musnad al- Dārimī*

The Classification of Hadith

In the early generations, during the time of the Companions of the Prophet, it was quite easy to know the Sunnah of the Prophet ﷺ because the Companions had witnessed him directly. Unfortunately, in the generations that followed, some people would make false attributions to the Prophet ﷺ and claim that he said things which he had not said.

They would do this with different intentions and agendas. This led to the scholars of Hadith putting an impressive amount of effort into preserving the Sunnah and distinguishing between authentic reports and false ones. They would study chains of narrations, the biographies of hadith narrators, and the texts of hadith in order to conclude which reports can comfortably be attributed to the Prophet ﷺ. Volumes have been written about those who narrated hadith so that we are able to know who the reliable and unreliable transmitters of hadith are. This effort was a collective one by many of the greatest scholars of Hadith, ensuring that the Sunnah of the Prophet ﷺ was preserved so that the Muslims may act upon it as Allah commanded them in the Qur'an.

This effort to study the Prophetic Traditions resulted in the formation of the science of Hadith. This became one of the most important of the Islamic sciences. It discusses chains of narration, different types of ahadith, the conditions for an authentic hadith, the different methods of transmitting hadith, the *fiqh* (understanding) of ahadith, and other relevant areas. Separate books have been authored in this science, known as *uṣūl al-ḥadīth* or *muṣṭalaḥ al-ḥadīth*, from the fourth century onwards. Some prominent works in this field include, *Ma'rifat 'Ulūm al-Ḥadīth* by Ḥākim al-Naysābūrī (d. 405 AH) and *Ma'rifat Anwā' 'Ulūm al-Ḥadīth* by Imam Abū 'Amr ibn al-Ṣalāḥ (d. 643 AH).

Studying the sciences of Hadith is an essential part of Islamic studies. We can only understand the Qur'an and the Shariah if we have a strong grounding in the sciences of Hadith and a good understanding of the *fiqh* of Hadith.

However, Hadith studies is usually a subject for the most dedicated of learners because it requires attention to detail. For instance, there are many classifications and categories of Hadith. Advanced readers can refer to the *Muqaddimah* by Ibn Ṣalāḥ which is also available in English. Readers who have access to Arabic can refer to many resources such as *al-Irshād* by al-Nawawī (which he later summarised in his

Taqrīb), al-Suyūṭī's *Tadrīb al-Rāwī,* Ibn Kathīr's *Ikhtiṣār 'Ulūm al-Ḥadīth*, al-Zarkashī's *al-Nukat,* al-'Iraqi's *al-Taqyīd wa al-Īḍāḥ* and Ibn Ḥajar al-'Asqalānī's *Nukhbat al-Fikr*.

As a beginner, you should know that scholars have made four major classifications of hadith based on the soundness of the hadith in terms of the reliability and memory of its reporters:

1. *Ṣaḥīḥ* (rigorously authentic)
2. *Ḥasan* (good)
3. *Ḍa'īf* (weak)
4. *Mawḍū'* (fabricated)

Ṣaḥīḥ (rigorously authentic)

This is defined by Ibn Ṣalāḥ as a hadith which has a continuous chain of narrators (*isnād*), who have narrated the hadith from only trustworthy (*thiqah*) narrators (those with perfect memory and uprightness) and it (the hadith) is free from irregularities (in the text) and defects (in the *isnād*). Such as: Mālik—from Nāfi'—from 'Abdullāh ibn Umar.

Ḥasan (good)

Al-Tirmidhī defines *ḥasan* as a hadith which is not irregular (*shādh*) nor contains a disparaged reporter in its chain of narrators, and is reported through more than one channel. Examples of *ḥasan* ahadith are those which have been reported by: 'Amr ibn Shu'ayb—from his father—from his grandfather or Muḥammad ibn 'Amr—from Abū Salamah—from Abū Hurayrah.

Ḍa'īf (weak)

A weak hadith is a hadith which has failed to meet the standard of *ṣaḥīḥ* or *ḥasan*. It is usually one that has faults in the continuity of the chain of narrators (*isnād*) or has a fault in a narrator in terms of lack of reliability either in memory or uprightness.

Mawḍūʿ (fabricated)

These are ahadith which the Prophet Muhammad ﷺ never said, but due to personal motives, were fabricated and attributed to him. A fabricated hadith can be detected either because one of the narrators is known to be a liar or because the text is of an obnoxious nature, thus going against the principles of Islam. For example, it is (falsely) attributed to the Prophet Muhammad ﷺ that he said, 'A negro will fornicate when his belly is full and steal when he is hungry.' This is fabricated due to its obnoxious nature, hence going against the noble character of the Prophet Muhammad ﷺ.

Oftentimes though, the wordings of a fabricated hadith may be non-offensive or even sound sensible. For example, 'To return one *dāniq* (a sixth of a dirham) to its owner is better than worshipping (Allah) for seventy years.' At such instances, scrutinising the hadith based on the thoroughly developed science of hadith classification would help us determine if it was in fact narrated by the Prophet Muhammad ﷺ or simply made up and falsely attributed to him.

1

The Fundamentals of Islam

عَنِ ابْنِ عُمَرَ رضي الله عنه قَالَ قَالَ رَسُولُ اللَّهِ ﷺ :بُنِيَ الإِسْلاَمُ عَلَى خَمْسٍ
شَهَادَةِ أَنْ لاَ إِلَهَ إِلاَّ اللَّهُ وَأَنَّ مُحَمَّدًا رَسُولُ اللَّهِ وَإِقَامِ الصَّلاَةِ وَإِيتَاءِ
الزَّكَاةِ وَالْحَجِّ وَصَوْمِ رَمَضَانَ

'Abdullāh ibn Umar رضي الله عنه narrated that the Prophet ﷺ said: 'Islam is built on five pillars: To testify that there is no god but Allah and Muhammad is the Messenger of Allah; to dutifully offer the prayers; to pay zakat; to perform hajj, and to fast the month of Ramadan.'

Islam, like other religions, has a set of values and principles which it demands its followers to uphold. In this hadith, narrated by 'Abdullāh ibn Umar, the Prophet Muhammad ﷺ teaches Muslims the core and fundamental aspects of Islam. These practices and rituals represent the religion which cannot be ignored, dismissed, or denied.

It is interesting to note that Prophet Muhammad ﷺ used the word *bu-ni-ya,* or 'built', to describe the fundamentals of Islam. A strong house needs to be built upon a foundation and must have a core which upholds its structure, without which the building will collapse and fall. The same notion can be applied when talking about Islam. In other words, it is not enough for a person to say 'I believe in Islam' without adhering to the values of Islam. Anyone who wishes to do so is living Islam in a distorted manner and not as it ought to be. This is why the expression *bu-ni-ya* or 'built' is best translated as 'pillars' because like a house which needs a foundation and pillars without which the structure will collapse, the religion of Islam also has a set of pillars, and if these pillars are not upheld then a person has not truly established Islam.

There are five pillars of Islam and the first and foremost of these pillars is the belief in monotheism: to believe in One God and that He alone should be worshipped. One cannot be considered a Muslim without also believing in the Prophet Muhammad ﷺ as the last and final Messenger of Allah. This declaration of faith, i.e., that there is no God but Allah, and Muhammad is the Messenger of Allah, is the ultimate verbal expression of faith in Islam.

The second pillar that the Prophet Muhammad ﷺ mentions is establishing the prayers. 'Establishing prayer' implies that it isn't enough for us to pray as and when we desire or when it is convenient for us. Rather, it refers to being dutiful in offering our prayers daily and on time—an act that is highly pleasing to Allah.

Third, giving the zakat, i.e., to give money to the poor and needy. Zakat and prayer are almost always mentioned together. This shows us the importance of both these pillars. What's fascinating is the literal meaning of the term 'zakat'—to purify. This word carries with it the subtle implication that it is only when we give our obligatory charity that our wealth and financial assets will be 'purified' and 'clean'.

Another pillar mentioned in the hadith is fasting, which is to abstain from food and water from sunrise to sunset. Every Muslim who has reached puberty is obliged to fast during the month of Ramadan as an expression of our sacrifice of pleasure and comfort for the sake of Allah, Most High.

Finally, hajj—the pilgrimage which Allah commands all Muslims who are able, physically and financially, to perform. It is to re-enact the great sacrifice that Prophet Ibrahim ﷺ and his wife, Hajar ؅, made for the pleasure of Allah.

This hadith teaches us the fundamentals of Islam, its core spiritual institutions and the greatest insignias of Allah's religion. A Muslim who fails to observe these five pillars has failed to reap the full benefits of Islam, whereas a Muslim who observes them can expect to achieve closeness to Allah and to receive His favours in this life and the next.

2

Modesty is a Part of Faith

عَنْ سَالِمِ بْنِ عَبْدِ اللَّهِ عَنْ أَبِيهِ أَنَّ رَسُولَ اللَّهِ ﷺ مَرَّ عَلَى رَجُلٍ
مِنَ الأَنْصَارِ وَهُوَ يَعِظُ أَخَاهُ فِي الْحَيَاءِ فَقَالَ رَسُولُ اللَّهِ ﷺ دَعْهُ
فَإِنَّ الْحَيَاءَ مِنَ الإِيمَانِ

'Abdullāh ibn Umar ؓ narrated: 'Once Allah's Messenger ﷺ passed by an Anṣārī who was admonishing his brother regarding modesty (*ḥayā'*). Upon that the Messenger of Allah ﷺ said, "Let him continue (his admonishment) as modesty is a part of faith."

Islam is a religion of balance. It not only came to teach us the ritual worship of Allah Most High, but also to provide a holistic provision for our welfare. Physical acts of worship devoid of morals and ethics leave humanity with a shortfall in their social dealings and conduct with others. Therefore, it is no surprise that Prophet Muhammad ﷺ

spent a lot of his time not only teaching his followers how to worship Allah, but also addressed codes of morality and ethics that we must exercise in relation to one another.

Many ahadith demonstrate how much the Prophet Muhammad ﷺ emphasised the importance of modesty. Once, he was walking with some of his Companions when he came across a man who was from the Anṣār[1]. The Anṣārī man was busy scolding someone else regarding modesty. The hadith suggests that the Anṣārī man's tone may have been slightly harsh. If it was excessive in harshness, the Prophet Muhammad ﷺ would have interjected, but he did not. Instead, he told his Companions to leave him as he was justified in his manner of admonishing the other. This suggests that the tone of telling off the other person was appropriate. Furthermore, the point of the Prophet ﷺ telling his Companions to leave them was to show his encouragement and support in the promotion of modesty.

It is worth noting that absence of modesty does not mean absence of faith. Indeed, a person who lacks modesty or has no modesty can still be a believer in Allah and His Messenger ﷺ. However, the purpose of linking modesty with faith means that the fruits of faith cannot be fully realised in the absence of modesty. Connecting modesty with faith reflects its importance in a Muslim's life. Ibn Qutaybah, a famous scholar of Hadith, comments on this, saying, 'Modesty prevents committing sin.'[2] It is obvious that when a person loses all sense of shame, there are no limits to what they can do. It is only faith infused with modesty which brings out the nobility of good character in a Muslim.

1 This is an honorific title given to the early Muslims of Madinah who helped the Prophet Muhammad ﷺ and gave the Muslims a home in Madinah.

2 Ibn Qutaybah, *Gharīb al-Hadīth*, vol. 1, p. 365

3

The Best of Deeds

عَنْ عَبْدِ اللَّهِ بْنِ عَمْرٍو ﵄ أَنَّ رَجُلاً سَأَلَ النَّبِيَّ ﷺ أَيُّ الإِسْلاَمِ خَيْرٌ قَالَ تُطْعِمُ الطَّعَامَ وَتَقْرَأُ السَّلاَمَ عَلَى مَنْ عَرَفْتَ وَمَنْ لَمْ تَعْرِفْ

'Abdullāh ibn 'Amr ﵄ narrated: 'A man once asked the Prophet ﷺ, "What sort of deeds (or what qualities) of Islam are the best?" The Prophet ﷺ replied, "To feed and to greet with *salām*, those whom you know and those whom you do not know."'

We all aspire to be the best in our particular field. For example, a chef wishes to be the best at cooking and at creating new dishes; an architect wants to be the best at designing new buildings; a teacher wants to be the best by virtue of his or her students enjoying the lessons; and so on. Islam champions this type of attitude. It is for this reason that the Prophet's Companions asked him what a person has to do in order to become the best Muslim.

The Prophet Muhammad ﷺ replied to the questioner that the best quality a person can possess is to feed someone. In this context, feeding someone does not mean to only feed the poor. There is no doubt about the nobility of feeding the poor, but the Prophet Muhammad ﷺ was talking about feeding people, in general. This includes relatives, guests, friends, colleagues, neighbours, and the likes. Sharing food and treating people to meals have an amazing ability to build strong relationships. Food is far more than fuel for the body; eating together and sharing food with one another is a social experience that makes us human, not to mention, one of life's great pleasures. Remember, the best Muslim is the one whose hands and tongue other Muslims are safe from. Nothing says more about peace and love than treating someone to food.

Similarly, the Prophet Muhammad ﷺ commanded us to greet others with the greetings of peace. This is an amazing way of informing the people we meet that we mean no harm and instead wish only peace and blessings for them. Imagine walking down the street and a stranger passing by says to you, 'peace be upon you'. Would it not make you feel immediately at ease? Would it not reassure you that they intend no harm towards you? Surely, it will give you a sense of friendship and safety. It is sad that nowadays, we greet only those whom we are previously acquainted with. It almost seems strange and out of place to say hello to a stranger. On the contrary, Islam teaches and in fact, encourages us to greet not only those whom we know, but also those whom we do not know, so as to spread the message of love and peace far and wide.

4

Beware of the Signs of a Hypocrite

عَنْ أَبِي هُرَيْرَةَ عَنِ النَّبِيِّ ﷺ قَالَ آيَةُ الْمُنَافِقِ ثَلاَثٌ إِذَا حَدَّثَ كَذَبَ وَإِذَا وَعَدَ أَخْلَفَ وَإِذَا اؤْتُمِنَ خَانَ

Abū Hurayrah ﵁ reported that the Prophet ﷺ said: 'The signs of a hypocrite are three: when he speaks, he lies; whenever he promises, he always breaks it; and if you entrust him, he proves to be dishonest.'

In Islam, a hypocrite is considered to be one of the worst categories of people. The Qur'an has clearly condemned such people to the extent that Allah has dedicated an entire surah exposing their behaviour. This surah talks about the result these people will suffer in the Hereafter. Allah says: *'Surely the hypocrites shall be in the lowest depth of the fire and you shall find none to come to their help'* (*al-Nisā'* 4: 145).

The technical definition of a hypocrite is a person who claims to be a Muslim openly but secretly is not, and instead, they conspire to harm

Islam and the Muslims. The Qur'an's condemnation is regarding such people. This hadith, however, does not refer to this type of hypocrite. Rather, the hadith implies that the holder of the three attributes mentioned are *like* hypocrites.

Integrity is a key component of the identity of an individual regardless of gender and social status. Honesty is a standalone virtue which speaks for itself and requires no explanation as to why it is virtuous. In fact, even a dishonest person appreciates an honest person, and in like manner, takes offence when labelled as dishonest.

This hadith specifically talks about lying, breaking a promise, and deceit, which is interesting because it suggests that the words of a hypocrite are faulty, their deeds are faulty, and their intentions are faulty. The hadith further provides us with two major benefits.

Firstly, the Prophet Muhammad ﷺ informed us of the three signs of a hypocrite. By knowing these signs, we can look for such traits within ourselves and change them.

Secondly, the hadith is a warning for us to be cautious when these attributes become evident in those around us. Being cautious does not necessarily mean to ostracise the persons in question, but to be wary of getting influenced by their traits of hypocrisy. It would then become a duty upon us, as well-wishing fellow Muslims, to help them with their problems by gently advising them to change their ways and by praying for them. It is only when they refuse help and are adamant about their behaviour, that we must take active measures to distance ourselves from their company, without giving up our prayers for them.

It is important to point out that ones intention is the key factor in understanding this hadith. That is to say, the signs of hypocrisy are true for a person who intentionally commits the aforementioned actions. This means, that when a person speaks, he intentionally lies with the aim of misleading, and when he promises something, he makes the intention to break it and when he is entrusted with something he intends on betraying that trust.

Breaking a promise is seriously blameworthy. If you promise to do something you must honour it. Allah says in the Qur'an, when He was talking about the righteous, '*...those who fulfil their promise when they promise*' (*al-Baqarah* 2:177). In another verse Allah explicitly lays down the moral obligation of honouring a promise, '*And fulfil [every] commitment. Indeed, the commitment is something you will be questioned about*' (*Bani Israil* 17:34). Although breaking a promise is a profound sin, making the intention not to keep a promise at the time of making it is even worse. It is a sign of hypocrisy. The same applies to a trust, either something said to someone in confidence to keep as a secret or an item left in the trust of someone. If a person breaks a trust, it is a major sin, but when a person receives this trust and at the time of receiving it intends on breaking it, then it is even worse. It is a sign of hypocrisy. Everyone knows lying is wrong, yet these traits have become very common among people nowadays. Everyone needs to know that they will have a reckoning in front Allah, and they have to account for all of their deeds, whether said or done. The question is, would you be included among the worst of people in front of Allah?

Avoiding Urine and Gossiping

عَنِ ابْنِ عَبَّاسٍ قَالَ مَرَّ النَّبِيُّ ﷺ بِقَبْرَيْنِ فَقَالَ إِنَّهُمَا لَيُعَذَّبَانِ وَمَا يُعَذَّبَانِ فِي كَبِيرٍ أَمَّا أَحَدُهُمَا فَكَانَ لاَ يَسْتَتِرُ مِنَ الْبَوْلِ وَأَمَّا الآخَرُ فَكَانَ يَمْشِي بِالنَّمِيمَةِ

Ibn 'Abbās ﷺ narrated: 'The Prophet ﷺ once passed by two graves and said, "These two persons are being tortured not for major sins. One of them never saved himself from being soiled with his urine, while the other used to go about with calumnies (to make enmity between friends)."'

Sometimes we make the mistake of thinking that mundane actions do not have consequences. However, what may seem mundane, often turns out to be a major issue. Every single action and saying has a profound effect on our spiritual and mental well-being, both on an individual and societal level. Islam always promotes the holistic welfare of people. In fact, it is from the objectives of the Shariah (*maqāṣid al-sharī'ah*) to preserve the intellect, wealth, soul, lineage, and religion; and anything that is proven to be harmful for human beings, should be actively removed.

Once, the Prophet Muhammad ﷺ was walking in Madinah and happened to pass by two graves. He stopped because he heard human-like voices coming from the graves. He turned to his Companions and informed them that the inhabitants of the graves were suffering punishment, not on account of major sins such as disbelief, murder, fornication or the likes of it, but on account of their minor sins. The Prophet Muhammad ﷺ said that one of the inhabitants of the grave was being punished for disregarding the rules of purity after using the toilet. Perhaps, the person thought that his action of being careless and not safeguarding himself from urine was a minor issue, and therefore not worthy of taking precaution and care. Perhaps, he would offer his prayers with defiled clothes. This hadith drives home the fact that urine is impure and must be cleaned, and that we must pay due diligence after using the privy and ensure to the best of our ability that impurities have been removed.

The inhabitant of the other grave also didn't think too much of his acts of tale-bearing. The consequence of his sin caused much rancour and upset. It is obvious why these two actions displeased Allah and how they contradicted the laws of Islam.

In the hope of helping the two in the grave, the Prophet ﷺ instructed one of his Companions to get him some branches off a tree. He then broke one into two and inserted them into the ground, telling his inquisitive Companions that as long as these branches remain fresh and do not wilt away, the inhabitants of the graves will be reprieved from punishment.

The circumstance of these two inhabitants of the grave serves as a warning to all of us. We learn that when someone constantly remains in a state of impurity, it will have an effect on their physical and spiritual well-being. Similarly, when a person has a habit of spreading tales and rancor, it will harm none but their own heart and character. On the whole, this hadith teaches us to be mindful of our deeds, as what may seem to be a minor sin can turn out to be a major sin, if we become complacent about it.

6

Food at the Time of Prayer

عَنْ عَائِشَةَ أن النَّبِيِّ ﷺ قَالَ إِذَا وُضِعَ الْعَشَاءُ وَأُقِيمَتِ الصَّلاَةُ
فَابْدَءُوا بِالْعَشَاءِ

'Ā'ishah ﵂ narrated that the Prophet ﷺ said: 'If supper is served, and *iqāmah* is pronounced, then start with the supper.'

Allah has created us in the best form, and it was by design—not accident—that He created us with flaws and weaknesses. Allah tells us in the Qur'an: *'And We have created humankind weak'* (*al-Nisā'* 4: 28). The purpose of having weaknesses is to test us, to see who amongst us is capable of controlling ourselves. Basic human desires are the primary point of such weaknesses.

One of our basic and most important needs is food. When the pangs of hunger kick in, it becomes difficult to concentrate on anything and it makes us grumpy and agitated. We may witness this phenomenon during the fasting month of Ramadan, when everyone experiences hunger, and everyone misses food for the duration of the fast. So, what should we do when both food and the time to pray coincide? The advice of the Prophet Muhammad ﷺ is clear: to eat first and then pray, even if we can hear the Imam recite the call for prayer. Ibn 'Umar ﵄ used to follow this advice. When he was presented with the dilemma of whether to eat first or pray, he would eat first and only after he finished, would he stand to offer his prayer.

Despite prayer being such an important part of Islam and a fundamental daily ritual, the Prophet ﷺ instructed Muslims to eat first and then pray. The reason for this is simple: if someone is hungry and food is present, it is likely that they would rush the prayer because their minds would be occupied with the thought of food. The prayer will therefore be devoid of focus, meditation, and concentration.

Scholars of Hadith have pointed out that the Prophet Muhammad's instruction here is an advice in terms of what is *better* to do. It does not mean that we cannot or must not pray first and then eat. Some scholars have concluded that the context of this hadith suggests that we should only eat before prayer if we are extremely hungry. So if you are only slightly hungry, and prayer has started, you should attend the prayer first. In like manner, if the food will go off or cannot be reheated if it is not eaten straightaway, then it is better to eat first and then pray. It is noteworthy that if you are afraid of the prayer time ending if you engage with food first, you should pray first and then eat.

This hadith teaches us the importance of praying with full concentration and devotion. The idea of prayer is to allow us to attain closeness to Allah, to help us be mindful of Allah, and grow in the love of Allah. When the mind is distracted, it cannot achieve this. This is why it is better to eat first and then pray.

7

Follow the Imam

قال رسول الله ﷺ إِنَّمَا جُعِلَ الإِمَامُ لِيُؤْتَمَّ بِهِ فَإِذَا رَكَعَ فَارْكَعُوا وَإِذَا رَفَعَ فَارْفَعُوا

The Prophet ﷺ said: 'The Imam is to be followed: bow when he bows, raise up your heads (stand upright) when he raises his head.'

Prayer in congregation is a truly beautiful scene to witness. This is especially so in the case of mass congregations such as the prayers at the Kaaba in Makkah, where hundreds and thousands of people pray in congregation under the command and instruction of one man, the Imam. It teaches Muslims discipline, obedience, and the importance of following instructions. When Muslims offer their prayer in congregation five times a day, this message is repeated with the aim of instilling a sense of discipline, propriety, and obedience to the person in charge.

In this hadith, the Prophet Muhammad ﷺ taught Muslims that the instructions of the Imam must be obeyed. It is neither valid nor permissible for a person praying in congregation to do anything before the Imam. When the Imam instructs the followers to proceed to bowing, they bow, and when he instructs them to prostrate, they prostrate.

As humans, we are endowed with freewill, and we have the tendency to do what we want and what we are convinced is the best course of action. On an individual level, this is laudable. We have the right to make decisions regarding our personal affairs and do what we think is best for us. However, in a group scenario, or when it affects many people, decision-making takes another dimension.

What is important is that decision-makers are respected, and their decisions are honoured, observed and duly implemented even if we do not agree with them. This is with the exception of vice or unlawful activities which are clearly mentioned in the Qur'an and hadith. In such a case, if we are ordered to do something Islamically wrong, it is our responsibility to not only refuse it but to also take a moral and ethical stand against it. The same is true in the case of prayer, where if the Imam does something incorrect, the followers are not allowed to follow him, instead they are responsible to correct him in prayer.

This hadith clearly teaches us the importance of following instructions. If legitimate leadership is ignored and everyone does as they please, it will cause disorder and chaos, whereas Islam aims to establish peace, order, and a smooth functioning of society.

8

Being Respectful of the Dead

عَنْ عَائِشَةَ قَالَتْ قَالَ النَّبِيُّ ﷺ لاَ تَسُبُّوا الأَمْوَاتَ فَإِنَّهُمْ قَدْ أَفْضَوْا إِلَى مَا قَدَّمُوا

'Ā'ishah ﵂ narrated that the Prophet ﷺ said: 'Do not curse the dead, for they have reached the result of what they have done.'

Death is the inevitable end for all of us, and our dealings with people will determine how we are remembered long after we are gone. What we say about others and how we treat them during our time on Earth will surely have an impact on us, not only in this world but in the Hereafter too. This is why Islam stresses on the importance of dealing with people compassionately and with good character. The Prophet Muhammad ﷺ said, 'And deal with people with good character.'[3]

3 Al-Tirmidhi, Sunan al-Tirmidhi, Hadith No. 1987

In this hadith, the Prophet Muhammad ﷺ wanted to teach Muslims to avoid insulting the dead. Perhaps someone who has been hurt by another feels immediate comfort in cursing the latter once they hear of their passing away. The Prophet Muhammad ﷺ extolled us to show restraint from such an urge. Some scholars like Ibn Rashīd said that it is neither permissible to curse the dead Muslim nor the dead non-Muslim. Ibn Baṭṭāl, another great Hadith scholar, points out that talking about the dead is akin to backbiting and therefore should be avoided.

There is no benefit to the living in insulting the dead, except that it may provide a temporary avenue to vent frustration and anger. It is better to either forgive the dead for which we will be rewarded, or if we cannot find it in our heart to forgive, wait to settle the dispute in front of Allah Most High, on the Day of Reckoning. What the Prophet Muhammad ﷺ is trying to teach us is that what the dead have committed cannot be reversed and therefore there is no point in insulting them. It is better to let Allah, the Most Just, deal with it. Maybe Allah will forgive them and reward us with something much better to compensate our loss.

9

Having Good Friends

عن أَبِي مُوسَى الأشعرى ﵁ قَالَ قَالَ رَسُولُ اللَّهِ ﷺ مَثَلُ الْجَلِيسِ الصَّالِحِ وَالْجَلِيسِ السَّوْءِ كَمَثَلِ صَاحِبِ الْمِسْكِ وَكِيرِ الْحَدَّادِ لاَ يَعْدَمُكَ مِنْ صَاحِبِ الْمِسْكِ إِمَّا تَشْتَرِيهِ أَوْ تَجِدُ رِيحَهُ وَكِيرُ الْحَدَّادِ يُحْرِقُ بَدَنَكَ أَوْ ثَوْبَكَ أَوْ تَجِدُ مِنْهُ رِيحًا خَبِيثَةً

Abū Mūsā al-Ashʿarī ﵁ narrated that the Messenger of Allah ﷺ said: 'The example of a good companion (who sits with you) in comparison with a bad one, is like that of the musk seller and the blacksmith's bellows (or furnace); from the first you would either buy musk or enjoy its good smell while the bellows would either burn your clothes or your house, or you get a bad smell thereof.'

There can be no doubt that our environment and surroundings have an effect on both our physical as well as psychological well-being. Consider this, when you enter a meat shop, do you expect it to smell of perfume? Do you expect that the butcher will smell of anything other than raw meat? When you enter a mechanic's workshop, do you expect things to be clean and tidy? Do you expect the mechanic to be clean and tidy? In both cases, and many more examples like them, we can see that the environment has an effect on the place and the person concerned. Similarly, the environment we work in has an effect on our personality as well.

We, humans, cannot subsist without other humans; our existence depends on working in cooperation with others. Allah, Most High, has created us as social creatures. This means that we need the company of other people to facilitate a better existence as well as to provide a better socio-mental well-being.

In fact, one of the most influential factors which shape our character is the friends we keep because they influence many aspects of our lives such as what we wear, where we go, where we eat, and so on.

It is therefore no surprise that the Prophet Muhammad ﷺ, knowing all too well the powerful influence friends have on a person, warned us about having bad friends and unhealthy companionships.

The beautiful thing about this hadith is that it is not age-centric. It applies to all age groups, and it is an advice of guidance for parents to remind their children, siblings to remind each other, teachers to remind their students, and Imams to remind the congregation they serve. The person reminding others also reminds themself of the danger of having bad companionship. Bad friends only lead to one thing: destruction. No good is ever bought about by having bad companions.

Let's take for example the story of the Prophet Nuh ﷺ and his son to show us how having bad friends can have devasting consequences. It is clear from the Qur'an that Prophet Nuh ﷺ loved his son very much. Despite having a father who was one of the greatest Prophets of

Allah, a father who was so gentle and loving, the influence of his bad friends made him blind to the truth. As a result of this, Prophet Nuh's son rejected faith and even when the storm started, his son was blind from seeing the truth. Allah tells us the story from the point when the rainstorm started, Prophet Nuh 鑿 said:

'Embark therein, in the Name of Allah will be its moving course and its resting anchorage. Surely, my Lord is Oft-Forgiving, Most Merciful. So, it (the ship) sailed with them amidst the waves like mountains, and Nuh called out to his son, who had separated himself, 'O my son! Embark with us and be not with the disbelievers.'

The son replied: 'I will betake myself to a mountain, it will save me from the water.' Nuh said: 'This day there is no saviour from the Decree of Allah except him on whom He has mercy.' And a wave came in between them, so he (the son) was among the drowned.' (*Hud* 11:45-47)

It is a guaranteed fact that bad friends will lead you to bad and good friends will lead you to good. It is your responsibility to choose your friends carefully.

10

Marriage and What to Do if you Cannot Get Married

قَالَ لَنَا النَّبِيُّ ﷺ يَا مَعْشَرَ الشَّبَابِ مَنِ اسْتَطَاعَ مِنْكُمُ الْبَاءَةَ
فَلْيَتَزَوَّجْ وَمَنْ لَمْ يَسْتَطِعْ فَعَلَيْهِ بِالصَّوْمِ فَإِنَّهُ لَهُ وِجَاءٌ

The Prophet ﷺ once said to us: 'O young people! Whoever among you is able to marry, should marry; and whoever is not able to marry, is recommended to fast, as fasting acts as a shield.'

One of the reasons Allah has created us is so that we can populate the Earth and act as His vicegerents. Regarding the creation of humankind, Allah says in the Qur'an: *'Indeed I will make a vicegerent on Earth'* (*al-Baqarah* 2: 30). Allah created humankind to worship Him and to procreate and be large in numbers. He created and fashioned humankind in the best manner and created for us desires and basic instincts for survival. It is from the perfection of Allah's religion and His mercy that for every human desire, He has made a lawful means to achieve it. For hunger, Allah has made halal food. To guard against the weather and protect modesty, Allah has made clothes. For the desire of wealth, Allah has created hard work and lawful gains. For sexual desire and procreation, Allah has created the institution of marriage.

Marriage is a vital social institution to preserve identity and link humankind into the global species it is. It is due to its significant status, namely preserving lineage, that marriage enjoys a special place in society and religion until today.

However, marriage is not an easy feat. It requires commitment, patience, understanding, maturity and financial ability. The urge to get married might start very early in humans. Puberty sparks this desire, which can begin as early as twelve years of age and even earlier in girls. At such an early age, although desires and physical ability might exist, it might not be the right time for a person to marry for many reasons such as mature-intelligence, education, and the like. It is due to this fact that not everyone will have the capacity to marry. The Prophet Muhammad ﷺ gave some excellent advice to his followers in this regard. He advised that those amongst us who have the means to marry in terms of physical ability, financial ability and temperament to deal with the spouse fairly, kindly, and with understanding and compassion, should not delay marriage. Those who are unable to do so because of, perhaps the aforementioned reasons, yet have sexual desires which need fulfilling, should resort to fasting. The lack of food will abate the natural urge and will divert the focus of the mind to other things.

This hadith teaches us the importance of marriage, keeping chaste and guarding our modesty, which will in turn benefit our emotional and psychological well-being. It provides those unable to marry with a temporary alternative until they overcome the obstacle and are able to marry.

Everyone Needs Good Neighbours

عَنْ أَبِى هُرَيْرَةَ عَنِ النَّبِيّ ﷺ قَالَ مَنْ كَانَ يُؤْمِنُ بِاللَّهِ وَالْيَوْمِ الآخِرِ فَلاَ يُؤْذِى جَارَهُ

Abū Hurayrah ؓ narrated that the Prophet ﷺ said: 'Whoever believes in Allah and the Last Day should not harm his neighbour.'

Everyone wishes to be treated nicely and with respect. Conversely, everyone finds being treated unkindly or disrespectfully to be an upsetting experience. Islam aims to create such a society where people are treated with respect and coexist in harmony, peace and safety. It has paid a great deal of attention to social and interpersonal codes of conduct, providing guidelines and instructions to help this process. Let's take, for example, greeting another person with 'peace be upon you', which is one of the oft-repeated greetings in Islam. It aims to foster and promote friendliness, fraternity, mutual love and respect.

It is further guided by principles that those that are younger should greet those that are older, the one entering a room should greet the one already present in the room, and the one standing should greet the one sitting. You can see that even the simplest of social interactions has advisory guidelines which aim to promote social cohesion.

Sometimes, it is easy for us to forget the rights others have over us. In other words, it is all too easy to be neglectful of such rights. Fortunately, Allah and His Messenger ﷺ have taught us the rights we have either *over* others or *towards* them. For example, a child's right over his or her parents is that they are provided with care, that they are raised in a safe and secure environment, and that they are nurtured with love and compassion. In like manner, the parents have rights over the child, in that the child should care for them in their old age, respect them, never raise their voice when addressing them and that they are generally loving and caring towards them. Similarly, Allah and His Messenger ﷺ have mentioned the rights people have over each other, such as the rights between husband and wife, brothers and sisters, uncles and nephews, friends and the like. One very important right, which may not seem obvious, is the right of neighbours.

Why did the Prophet Muhammad ﷺ emphasise so much on the rights of neighbours? Perhaps it is because the rights of parents, siblings, relatives and the like are generally known. Everyone knows that parents have rights over them, an older sibling knows he or she has a sense of duty toward the younger siblings, a student knows that the teacher must be honoured and respected, and so on. What may not be obvious are the tremendous rights neighbours have over each other. Often, living so closely with people means we can get in the way of each other—this is inevitable. Therefore, maintaining good ties with neighbours requires cooperation, understanding, patience, and tolerance.

Unfortunately, it is becoming a trend that the elderly and vulnerable are neglected and left to live alone. If you are aware of such people in your neighbourhood, then it is your responsibility to ensure they are well and safe. Causing any kind of harm to our neighbours is a sin so severe that it can block our entry into Paradise. Once the Prophet Muhammad ﷺ said, "By Allah, he does not have faith! By Allah, he does not have faith! By Allah, he does not have faith!" His Companions enquired, 'Who is it that does not have faith, O Messenger of Allah?' The Prophet said, "He whose neighbour is not safe from his harm."[4] In another hadith, the Prophet Muhammad ﷺ said, 'Whoever believes in Allah and the Last Day should honour his neighbours.'

When neighbours behave wrongly towards each other, life becomes miserable. This kind of behaviour goes against what Islam stands for and what it wants to promote. Therefore, we should take the rights of our neighbours very seriously, even if they are not Muslim. As we can see from this hadith, how we treat our neighbours is so important that it is a mark of our faith in Allah and the Last Day.[5]

4 Al-Bukhārī, *Ṣaḥīḥ al-Bukhārī*, Hadith No. 6016

5 Al-Bukhārī, *Ṣaḥīḥ al-Bukhārī*, Hadith No. 5672

Everyone Must Observe their Responsibility

عَنْ عَبْدِ اللَّهِ قَالَ النَّبِيُّ ﷺ كُلُّكُمْ رَاعٍ وَكُلُّكُمْ مَسْئُولٌ فَالإِمَامُ
رَاعٍ وَهْوَ مَسْئُولٌ وَالرَّجُلُ رَاعٍ عَلَى أَهْلِهِ وَهْوَ مَسْئُولٌ وَالْمَرْأَةُ
رَاعِيَةٌ عَلَى بَيْتِ زَوْجِهَا وَهْىَ مَسْئُولَةٌ

'Abdullāh ibn Umar رضي الله عنه narrated that the Prophet ﷺ said: 'Every one of you is a guardian and every one of you is responsible. A ruler is a guardian and is responsible (for his subjects); a man is a guardian of his family and responsible (for them); a wife is a guardian of her husband's house and she is responsible for it.'

'Blessed is Allah who is the best of creators' (*al-Mu'minūn* 23: 14).

Life on Earth has a purpose, and everything around us, everything we see, touch or smell has its own purpose and function, whether we understand it or not. When this purpose and function are fulfilled properly, there is harmony in the creation of Allah. For example, we know the function of the sun and moon. What would happen if these two did not carry out their roles properly?

Let's look at the functioning of the human body. Each organ, limb or cell has a role to play, and if even one element does not fulfil its role, it can lead to catastrophic repercussions. In like manner, Allah has designated roles and responsibilities for people, in order to ensure the smooth functioning of human society.

In this hadith, the Prophet Muhammad ﷺ teaches us that every person has a role and responsibility towards others. Having responsibilities means that people can be held accountable for the duties that Allah has assigned to them. The Prophet ﷺ used three groups of people to make this point clear.

He talks about the leader and outlines that their responsibility is to serve the people. How can it be that the leader lives in a multimillion-pound palace with full access to food, water, heating and security while the people suffer the hardship of hunger, want, and danger? Has such a leader lived up to their responsibility?

The Prophet Muhammad ﷺ then also talks about the husband and his responsibility towards his wife and children, that he should provide for them a safe place to stay, a roof over their heads, food on the table and clothes on their back. The money he earns is therefore the property of his family first and any amount left over is his.

In turn, the wife, the Prophet Muhammad ﷺ says, is responsible for looking after all the household affairs, maintaining it, taking care of it and protecting it. The responsibility of the parents is not only to provide provisions for the household, but to also create an environment full of love, happiness and affection. Removing this from any household will create weakness, illness and instability. When this happens, society suffers.

When everyone in society takes the concept of responsibility seriously and strives to fulfil their responsibility, it paves the way for prosperity, happiness and peace.

Having Gender Boundaries

عَنِ ابْنِ عَبَّاسٍ عَنِ النَّبِيِّ ﷺ قَالَ لاَ يَخْلُوَنَّ رَجُلٌ بِامْرَأَةٍ إِلاَّ مَعَ
ذِى مَحْرَمٍ

Ibn 'Abbās ☙ narrated that the Prophet ☙ said: 'No
man should stay with a woman in seclusion except in the
presence of a *mahram*.[6]'

Allah has created everything with wisdom and purpose. He has
placed within His creation the potential to fulfil its purpose,
alongside elements of strength and weakness. Let us take for example,
fire: its main purpose is to provide heat and it is a very powerful force.
Yet, this powerful force, which has the potential to destroy and wipe out
an entire city, is weak in the face of water. Let us look to the mountain
and marvel at its majestic construct, the grandeur of its presence, and

---

6   This term refers to a family member with whom marriage is forbidden and
    around whom hijab is not obligatory.

the formidable nature of its creation. Yet, it is weak in the face of iron which can be used to chisel away at the mountain. Iron is strong and durable, it is capable of carrying loads of hundreds and thousands of tonnes, yet it is weak in the face of fire, which can melt it into liquid.

Each of Allah's creations have a purpose, function and an in-built strength with which it lives up to its potential. Similarly, we humans have been created with the most noble of purposes and endowed with the strength needed to fulfil our potential. Having said that, we nevertheless suffer from many weaknesses as well. One of those weaknesses is our natural attraction to the opposite sex, the most sensitive and vulnerable of basic human instincts. Our level of piety has no bearing in this regard and it cannot be said, 'So-and-so is a religious person therefore he or she can be trusted.' Due to the sensitive nature and inherent weakness in humankind, Islam clearly expresses its opposition to any meeting between a man and woman taking place in seclusion.

The hadith highlights the serious weakness humans and in particular men suffer in this regard, and Islam has taken strict and clear measures to avoid giving Satan an opportunity to mislead us. There are many examples, current and past, where the lack of observing respectful boundaries has led to the abuse and mistreatment of women (and men).

There is no merit in the claim that men and women are expected to observe boundaries by themselves. It is clear and evident that this is a false notion. The weakness in men will always dominate any other sense of decorum and appropriateness; it is a weakness that is far too delicate to leave to wishful thinking and hoping that people *ought* to behave themselves. This hadith teaches us the importance of keeping away from temptation, protecting our integrity, and ensuring we do not fall victim to the plots of Satan.

It does not matter who you are; if you put yourself in a compromising situation, it is only a matter of time before Satan will find an opportunity to mislead you.

14

The Importance of Brotherhood

عَنْ أَبِي مُوسَى عَنِ النَّبِيِّ ﷺ قَالَ الْمُؤْمِنُ لِلْمُؤْمِنِ كَالْبُنْيَانِ يَشُدُّ بَعْضُهُ بَعْضًا ثُمَّ شَبَّكَ بَيْنَ أَصَابِعِهِ

Abū Mūsā al-Ashʿarī ﵁ narrated: 'The Prophet ﷺ said, "A believer to another believer is like a building whose different parts enforce each other." He then clasped his hands with the fingers interlaced.'

The idea of a religious fraternity is the cornerstone of Islam's inter and intra social cohesion agenda. Allah tells us in the Qur'an that all believers are brothers and sisters, and many ahadith repeat this idea and reinforce the concept of brotherhood/sisterhood in faith. For example, the Prophet Muhammad ﷺ said, 'A Muslim to another Muslim is his brother, therefore he does not wrong him or let him down."[7] Social discord creates instability, which leads to disunity, which in turn leads to weakness. Thereafter, weakness leads to destruction.

Unity is at the heart of the concept of ummah (community) in Islam. Allah commands the believers: *'And hold fast on to the rope of Allah and do not split'* (*Āl 'Imrān* 3: 103). In another hadith, the Prophet Muhammad ﷺ described the Muslim community as one body, and he continued by giving an example to show that empathy and sympathy must be felt by all Muslims towards each other. He said, "The parable of the believers in their affection, mercy, and compassion for each other is that of a body. When any limb aches, the whole body reacts with sleeplessness and fever."[8]

These ahadith teach us that we must stick together and not allow our differences to get in the way of a united front. Islam teaches Muslims that faith, that is to say, belief in Allah and His Messenger ﷺ, transcends cultural and racial boundaries. The colour, race, ethnicity, and gender of a believer has no significance whatsoever in Islam or in the Sight of Allah. Believers, regardless of these factors, are all brothers and sisters in faith. Just as it is a natural expectation that your brother or sister will always be by your side, ready to help and care for you at the time of need, the same should be expected from all Muslims all over the world. They must be ready to help another Muslim at the time of need, to care for them, and protect them from harm.

This hadith is more relevant to us now than ever before. Perhaps, previously Muslims could not see the oppression other Muslims experienced in the world, or those struck by abject poverty, or those who became victims of a natural disaster. However, now these experiences can be seen instantaneously and continuously. It remains the duty of Muslims who believe in Allah and His Messenger ﷺ to help

---

7 Muslim, *Sahih Muslim*, Hadith No. 2564

8 Al-Bukhārī, *Ṣaḥīḥ al-Bukhārī*, Hadith No. 6011, Muslim, *Ṣaḥīḥ Muslim,* Hadith No. 2586

all Muslims, wherever they may be. Is it not so, that by having social discord we have created instability and through this instability we have created disunity, and through this disunity we have created weakness, and this weakness is our current situation?

What all Muslims should do is learn to be tolerant towards each other, help each other and cooperate to form a single body. We should not become a community which identifies itself in terms of borders and boundaries but a single community which identifies itself as Muslims.

The Importance of Manners and Character

وعن عبد الله بن عمرو، قَالَ قَالَ رَسُولُ اللَّهِ ﷺ إِنَّ مِنْ أَخْيَرِكُمْ أَحْسَنَكُمْ خُلُقًا

'Abdullāh ibn 'Amr ﷺ reported that the Messenger of Allah ﷺ said: 'The best among you are those who have the best manners and character.'

When 'Ā'ishah ﷺ, the wife of the Prophet Muhammad ﷺ, was asked about his character she replied, 'He was the Qur'an, walking.' This should not be surprising in light of the fact that the Qur'an declares, *'And you are on an exalted standard of character'* (*al-Qalam* 68:4), and the Prophet Muhammad ﷺ himself said, 'I have been sent to perfect good character.' The fact that one of the mission objectives of the Prophet Muhammad ﷺ was to perfect good character, demonstrates the high status it has in Islam. Al-Qurṭubī says that being of good character is so important for the simple reason that it would reflect in the way a person behaves towards others. A person of good character will always behave properly towards his or her parents, brothers and sisters, neighbours, friends, relatives and so on. Someone who has improper behaviour towards others, is careless about committing sin, and shows no regard for the things around him or her, cannot claim to be of good character. Good character is the driving momentum that shapes our interaction and relationships with others, which is why Islam focuses and heavily emphasises on building the character of Muslims.

Part and parcel of good character is generosity. Another hadith describes the character of the Prophet Muhammad ﷺ as the most generous and the bravest of men. A common character deficiency we see in people (including ourselves) is miserliness. Perhaps the psychological satisfaction of seeing many numbers on our bank balance provides us with a feel-good factor and gives us a sense of security, which in turn makes us want to hold on to the money we have. We fear spending will decrease our wealth and cause it to finish. Although the Prophet ﷺ was not wealthy, he spent whatever he had on his family and the poor. Jābir ؓ narrates that the Prophet Muhammad ﷺ never said 'no' when asked for something to be given in charity.

This hadith teaches us the importance of good character. It is an attribute second to none. Having good character means that a person is forgiving, patient, understanding, generous, kind, and compassionate. Good character is not something we can learn by reading a book or by attending a course. Rather, it is a slow process of nurturing, which comes as a result of having good companionship with the righteous and pious. Every Muslim must make an earnest endeavour to perfect his or her character.

16

The Most Beloved to the Prophet Muhammad ﷺ

عن عَمْرُو بْنُ الْعَاصِ رضي الله عنه أَنَّ النَّبِيَّ ﷺ بَعَثَهُ عَلَى جَيْشِ ذَاتِ السَّلَاسِلِ۝ فَأَتَيْتُهُ فَقُلْتُ أَيُّ النَّاسِ أَحَبُّ إِلَيْكَ۝ قَالَ عَائِشَةُ فَقُلْتُ مِنَ الرِّجَالِ فَقَالَ أَبُوهَا قُلْتُ ثُمَّ مَنْ۝ قَالَ ثُمَّ عُمَرُ بْنُ الْخَطَّابِ

'Amr ibn al-'Āṣ رضي الله عنه narrated: 'The Prophet ﷺ deputed me to lead the Army of *Dhāt al-Salāsil*. I came to him and said, "Who is the most beloved person to you?" He said, "'Ā'ishah." I asked, "Among the men?" He said, "Her father." I said, "Who then?" He said, "Then Umar ibn al-Khaṭṭāb."'

Everyone needs a friend; someone we can rely on, someone we can share our problems with and someone who can give good advice. This is part of being human and is the reason why the Prophet Muhammad ﷺ encouraged us to seek out good friends. That is to say, if everyone needs friends to live a better and healthier life, then it is our duty to select good people to have as friends. The great Companion 'Amr ibn al-'Āṣ ﷺ was curious as to who the Prophet's best friend was. So, he asked him, perhaps hoping that the Prophet ﷺ would say it was him. We can assume this on account of two reasons: Firstly, when asked who he loves the most, the Prophet ﷺ replied it was 'Ā'ishah ﷺ, after which 'Amr ibn al-'Āṣ ﷺ clarified he meant from the Prophet's male acquaintances. Secondly, after the Prophet Muhammad ﷺ said the second person among his male acquaintances was Umar ibn al-Khaṭṭāb ﷺ, he continued to ask for a third and fourth person until he decided to stop, fearing that the Prophet Muhammad ﷺ might mention him as the last person.

All the Companions loved the Prophet Muhammad ﷺ and he loved them. It is natural for a person to become attached to those who helped them the most and to those who are committed with loyalty and devotion. His wife, 'Ā'ishah ﷺ was the first-mentioned person he loved. The intimate spousal relationship is the fundamental cause of this affection. She had a very special place in the Prophet's heart, so much so that the Prophet ﷺ wished to spend his very last days on Earth in the house of 'Ā'ishah ﷺ.

Abu Bakr ﷺ and Umar ﷺ never left the side of the Prophet Muhammad ﷺ and were at his constant beck and call. The commitment of Abu Bakr and Umar ﷺ and their love and devotion to the Prophet Muhammad ﷺ stands alone as evidence of their greatness in Islam.

Abu Bakr ﷺ was gentle in his nature and this made him closer to the Prophet's character and their friendship predated Islam. The Prophet Muhammad ﷺ once said about Abu Bakr ﷺ that he believed in him as the Messenger of Allah when everyone else belied him. When the Prophet Muhammad ﷺ invited people to Islam, everyone wanted to have some time think about it, had additional questions or opposed him initially—all but Abu Bakr رضي الله عنه. When the Prophet ﷺ invited him to accept Islam, Abu Bakr رضي الله عنه did so without hesitation or a second thought. This demonstrates the high level of trust and the solid foundation of friendship between them. Abu Bakr رضي الله عنه was his friend when everyone opposed him.

On the other hand, Umar رضي الله عنه was strict in his personality and could not tolerate any harm or wrong committed towards the Prophet ﷺ. He was a highly intelligent man and a great source of advice to the Prophet ﷺ in times of need. If any task needed to be done, Umar رضي الله عنه was there to carry it out.

This hadith teaches us that Abu Bakr and Umar رضي الله عنهما were the most beloved to the Prophet Muhammad ﷺ among his male Companions. Therefore, they must be revered by all Muslims at all times. It cannot be possible that these people, whom the Prophet Muhammad ﷺ loved so much would do something to hurt him. Moreover, if the Prophet ﷺ loved them, then all Muslims must also love them. How can a Muslim say they believe in Allah and His Messenger ﷺ and in the same breath say they dislike Abu Bakr and Umar رضي الله عنهما?

17

The Virtues of Teaching Qur'an

عَنْ عُثْمَانَ ﵁ عن النَّبِيِّ ﷺ قَالَ خَيْرُكُمْ مَنْ تَعَلَّمَ الْقُرْآنَ وَعَلَّمَهُ

Uthman ﵁ narrated that the Prophet ﷺ said: 'The best among you (Muslims) are those who learn the Qur'an and teach it.'

Education is crucial for personal development and something highly regarded by Islam. Without knowledge, we cannot worship Allah as we ought to or live our lives fulfilling the commandments of Allah. It is no accident that the very first word, the very first command and instruction Allah gave His beloved Messenger ﷺ was to 'read' (*iqra'*).

Learning is the key to the advancement of a nation while illiteracy is the cause of the destruction of a nation. Learning is not a one-day or one-year event; rather it is a lifelong process. Formal education at institutions of learning might come to an end at a certain point, but a true believer and a true seeker of knowledge knows that learning never ends.

In a fascinating hadith, the Prophet Muhammad ﷺ spoke about two greedy and insatiable people who are never satisfied with what they have: one, the Prophet ﷺ said, was a person who was greedy for worldly possessions; and the other was a person greedy for knowledge.

Once, the Prophet Muhammad ﷺ passed by two groups of people, one group was engaged in the remembrance of Allah (*dhikr*) and the other was engaged in the recitation of the Qur'an and learning. The Prophet ﷺ said that both groups were doing righteous deeds, but he chose to sit with those engaged in learning because he said he was sent as a teacher (*mu'allim*).

This hadith teaches us the importance of learning the Qur'an in terms of how to read it, what it means, and how to live according to its teachings. Living the Qur'an is our primary duty, after which it should be taught to others. The Prophet Muhammad ﷺ described those engaged in learning the Qur'an and those teaching it as the best. Learning Mathematics, Science, Languages, History and the like is praiseworthy no doubt, but nothing is more rewarding and virtuous in the Sight of Allah than those who learn the Qur'an and those who teach it.

Everyone aspires to be the best and desires to be recognised as the best. Imagine being seen as the best in the Sight of Allah and His Messenger ﷺ. On the Day of Judgement, mere degrees and qualifications in Mathematics, Science, Geography and History will be of no benefit, nor will they be of any use, in and of themselves. What will be of use and benefit to us is our deeds that involve learning the Qur'an and teaching it to others. However, if a person is not in a position to teach the Qur'an, then let him or her at least help those who are by supporting them financially and by praying for them.

18

The Etiquettes of Eating

عُمَرَ بْنَ أَبِي سَلَمَةَ يَقُولُ كُنْتُ غُلاَمًا فِي حَجْرِ رَسُولِ اللَّهِ ﷺ
وَكَانَتْ يَدِى تَطِيشُ فِي الصَّحْفَةِ فَقَالَ لِي رَسُولُ اللَّهِ ﷺ يَا غُلاَمُ
سَمِّ اللَّهَ وَكُلْ بِيَمِينِكَ وَكُلْ مِمَّا يَلِيكَ فَمَا زَالَتْ تِلْكَ طِعْمَتِي بَعْدُ

'Umar ibn Abī Salamah ﵁ narrated: 'I was a boy under the care of the Messenger of Allah ﷺ and my hand used to go around the dish while I was eating. So, the Messenger of Allah ﷺ said to me, "Young man, mention the Name of Allah and eat with your right hand, and eat of the dish what is nearer to you." Since then, I have applied those instructions when eating.'

Etiquettes, manners and codes of conduct are essential elements to the character of a person. It is these attributes by which people measure others. The Prophet ﷺ was sent not only to teach us how to worship Allah, but to teach us about all aspects of life as well. His teachings reveal the minute details of how to behave in all circumstances and what to do in different situations. He has taught his followers the basics such as how to brush their teeth and how to clean themselves after using the privy, and has also taught them more complex practicalities such as how to conduct themselves as judges and heads of states.

The narrator of the hadith is the son of Umm Salamah ؓ, the wife of the Prophet Muhammad ﷺ; therefore, he was the stepson of the Prophet ﷺ. 'Umar ؓ was only a young boy when he was living with the Prophet Muhammad ﷺ. Once, when eating, he went fishing around the plate taking all the best bits, and perhaps spoiling the rest of the food. In the best manner, with kindness and gentle words, the Prophet ﷺ corrected him and taught him the etiquettes of eating in a social context. The Prophet ﷺ gave him three instructions: the first was to mention Allah's Name (*bismillah*); the second was to eat with the right hand; and the third was to eat from that which was nearest to him.

In most Arab cultures, eating is a family and communal event, and it involves sitting together around one plate of food. If one person begins to take food from all parts of the plate, it would cause annoyance to the other people sharing the food. The etiquette therefore is to eat from what's nearest to the person.

It is noteworthy that when the Prophet Muhammad ﷺ chose to correct 'Umar ibn Abī Salamah ؓ, he not only pointed out to him his fault, but also built on it as a general part of teaching the child. Teaching must be done with gentleness and not with anger and frustration.

'Umar ؓ was dutiful to the instructions of the Prophet Muhammad ﷺ and said he never did otherwise from that day. In other words, he adhered to the teachings of the Prophet Muhammad ﷺ throughout his entire life from that day forward.

19

Character of a Muslim

عَنْ عَبْدِ اللَّهِ بْنِ عَمْرٍو رَضِىَ اللَّهُ عَنْهُمَا عَنِ النَّبِيِّ صَلَّى اللهُ عَلَيْهِ وَسَلَّمَ قَالَ المُسْلِمُ مَنْ سَلِمَ المُسْلِمُونَ مِنْ لِسَانِهِ وَيَدِهِ

'Abdullāh ibn 'Amr ﵄ narrated that the Prophet ﷺ said: 'The [true] Muslim is the one who avoids harming other Muslims with his tongue and hands.'

The purpose of Islam is to spread peace on a societal level, both nationally as well as internationally. It is for this reason that Muslims greet each other with the Arabic phrase '*assalāmu 'alaykum*' or 'peace be with you'. With respect to interpersonal relationships, one of the fundamental aims of Islam is to champion love and affection between members of a society. As humans, it is easy to let our emotions overcome us, and let our strength dictate the way we behave, especially against the weak. Addressing the code of conduct by which Muslims must live their lives, the Prophet Muhammad ﷺ outlined that a true

Muslim is the one who avoids harming other Muslims with their tongue and hands.

This hadith was in response to a question posed by the Companions to the Prophet Muhammad ﷺ. They asked him, 'O Messenger of Allah, what kind of Islam is the best?' What they meant by that was, 'What virtue of Islam in a person's character is best?' To this the Prophet ﷺ replied, 'The [true] Muslim is the one who avoids harming other Muslims with his tongue and hands.'

In this hadith, the Messenger of Allah ﷺ teaches Muslims that those who truly follow Islam properly are those who make sure they do not harm other people. This applies to any type of harm regardless of its shape and form. However, the two types of harm that were specifically emphasised in the hadith are harming people with the tongue and with the hand. Harming people with the tongue can include making fun of other people, teasing them, giving them mean and spiteful nicknames, backbiting them, and telling them things that may upset them. Muslims guilty of this type of behaviour need to stop and reflect on the teachings of the Prophet of Islam ﷺ. No one can claim that they are a true Muslim and be engaged in the aforementioned types of behaviour.

Allah also tells us in the Qur'an: *'O you who believe, let no people mock any other people'* (*al-Ḥujurāt* 49: 11). Although, the Prophet Muhammad ﷺ emphasised being kind to Muslim brothers and sisters in particular, this message is not exclusive to them. Rather, Muslims have been commanded to speak kindly to all people, whether they are Muslim or not. Allah Almighty says in the Qur'an: *'And speak to people with goodness'* (*al-Baqarah* 2: 83).

As well as being kind to people with our words, we must also make sure to never hurt anyone with our hands. This means to not hit anyone and to not take anything that does not belong to us. Our hands are a blessing from Allah that we should only use for good. Using them to hurt others would indicate that we are not truly grateful for this blessing, and when we become ungrateful, we do not appreciate the

One who has given us the gift of limbs.

The best of Muslims are those who never hurt others in any manner. It is important to remember this the next time we say or do something that may hurt another person.

20

Loving the Messenger of Allah ﷺ

عَنْ أَنَسٍ قَالَ قَالَ النَّبِيُّ صَلَّى اللهُ عَلَيْهِ وَسَلَّمَ لاَ يُؤْمِنُ أَحَدُكُمْ حَتَّى أَكُونَ أَحَبَّ إِلَيْهِ مِنْ وَالِدِهِ وَوَلَدِهِ وَالنَّاسِ أَجْمَعِينَ

Anas ﷺ reported that the Prophet ﷺ said: 'None of you shall truly believe until I become more beloved to him than his parents, children, and all of mankind.'

It is an essential part of Islam to place our love for the Prophet ﷺ above our love for any other human being, including ourselves. When Umar ibn al-Khaṭṭāb ﷺ heard the Messenger of Allah ﷺ say this, he stood up and said, 'O Messenger of Allah, I love you more than everything but myself.' The Prophet ﷺ replied, 'No, by Him in whose Hand is my soul, you have not believed until I am dearer to you than your own self.' Umar ﷺ paused, standing for a while, and then said, 'You are now dearer to me than my own self.' The Prophet ﷺ replied, 'Now (you have believed).' It should be noted that 'not believing' here means not reaching the perfection and excellence of faith and it does not imply that not having such a level of love for the Prophet Muhammad ﷺ is disbelief.

One of the easiest ways to enter Paradise is to fill our hearts with love for Prophet Muhammad ﷺ. But this can only be done if we know who he is and why he deserves our deepest love and reverence. It can also only be achieved if we place all our love with the Creator first. Only then can we truly love the Messenger of Allah ﷺ.

A man once came to the Prophet Muhmmad ﷺ and said, 'O Messenger of God, when is the Day of Judgment?' The Messenger ﷺ said, 'What have you prepared for it?' The man said, 'I have not really prepared much for it, except that I love Allah and His Messenger.' The Messenger ﷺ then said, 'You will be with those you love.'

So, why is it so important that Muslims should love Prophet Muhammad ﷺ more than anyone or anything else in the world? There are a number of reasons for this, but the two most important ones are: gaining closeness to Allah; and being grateful for Allah's mercy upon us by sending His final Messenger, Muhammad ﷺ to guide us to the straight path, without whom we would be far astray in this life. There is no greater blessing than guidance. We are extremely fortunate and should be grateful that Allah has guided us to the beautiful clear religion of Islam, while many others are oblivious to their purpose in life and have no source of guidance.

The sacrifices that Prophet Muhammad ﷺ made for the sake of delivering the message of Islam are beyond imaginable. He gave all that he had to convey the message of Allah as clearly as possible. Allah, Almighty tells us of this in the Qur'an: *'Today I have perfected your religion for you, and have completed My blessing upon you, and chosen Islam as a dīn (religion and way of life) for you'* (*al-Mā'idah* 5: 3).

The status that the Prophet ﷺ has been given is most fitting, much like the position that Islam grants parents. What makes our parents so worthy of our respect and honour? What makes them so deserving of our attention, care and love? It is the sacrifice they have made to bring us up. For them, we were their priority, and our well-being came before anything else, even before their own well-being. It is this sacrifice they made that makes them so deserving of our love and respect. In like manner, the sacrifice Prophet Muhammad ﷺ made for his followers was so great, that he has become deserving of this station. The Prophet ﷺ also wanted to teach Muslims loyalty and recognition for devotion, to teach us that there are more important things than ourselves.

21

The Virtue of Knowledge and Scholars

عَنْ عَبْدِ اللَّهِ بْنِ عَمْرِو بْنِ العَاصِ قَالَ سَمِعْتُ رَسُولَ اللَّهِ صَلَّى
اللهُ عَلَيْهِ وَسَلَّمَ يَقُولُ إِنَّ اللَّهَ لاَ يَقْبِضُ العِلْمَ انْتِزَاعًا يَنْتَزِعُهُ مِنَ
العِبَادِ وَلَكِنْ يَقْبِضُ العِلْمَ بِقَبْضِ العُلَمَاءِ حَتَّى إِذَا لَمْ يُبْقِ عَالِمًا
اتَّخَذَ النَّاسُ رُءُوسًا جُهَّالًا فَسُئِلُوا فَأَفْتَوْا بِغَيْرِ عِلْمٍ، فَضَلُّوا وَأَضَلُّوا

'Abdullāh ibn 'Amr ibn al-'Āṣ ﵄ said that he heard the Messenger of Allah ﷺ saying: 'Allah does not take away knowledge by taking it away from (the hearts of) the people, but takes it away by the death of the scholars, until no scholar remains. (Then) people will take as their leaders ignorant persons who when consulted will give their verdict without knowledge. So, they will go astray and will lead the people astray.'

Knowledge is the most powerful asset one can possess. It is knowledge that made Prophet Adam ﷺ outshine the angels. Allah taught Prophet Adam ﷺ and endowed him with knowledge that even the angels didn't have. When asked to mention the names of everything, the angels—who were foremost in obeying and worshipping Allah—failed to show their superiority in knowledge.[9] Prophet Adam ﷺ, on the other hand, answered every question right, and the angels bowed to him in honour and recognition as per Allah's command. Knowledge is respected by everyone, and everyone admires a knowledgeable person. It is the force that causes a nation to advance and excel. Therefore, Islam has emphasised heavily on the virtues of knowledge and the people of knowledge.

This hadith shows that true knowledge is the knowledge of the Scriptures and it belongs in the hearts of scholars. Allah, Almighty states: *'Indeed, they are clear verses in the hearts of those who have been given knowledge'* (*al-'Ankabūt* 29: 49). The Scriptures are sent in clear terms, but it has subtleties which not everyone can interpret. It requires the investment of time and selfless dedication to reach a level of understanding its intricate aspects. Without the correct skills, tutelage and knowledge, Scriptures can easily be misunderstood. This is the role of scholars who will clarify that which is unclear to the people. This itself shows the great status of the scholars of Islam; those who have knowledge of the Book of Allah and the teachings of the Messenger of Allah ﷺ. They take on the role of the Prophets in delivering the message of Islam, in explaining the Qur'an and Prophetic teachings, and in resolving the confusions and problems that exist amongst the Muslims. This is the reason why the Prophet Muhammad ﷺ said, 'The scholars are the heirs of the Prophets, and the Prophets leave neither dinar nor dirham (to be inherited), leaving only knowledge, and he

9 Jalāl al-Dīn al-Mahalli and al-Suyūtī, *Tafsir al-Jalalayn*, English translation, pp. 13-14

who takes it takes an abundant portion.'[10]

This hadith wants to teach us two things: firstly, to motivate people to seek knowledge; and secondly, to reach the level of excellence in scholarship for both men and women. This is because as the scholars pass away, there is a need to replace them and fill the gap of taking on the role of the Prophets in guiding people. Furthermore, the hadith informs us of a grim time when scholars pass away and nobody fills their space, which ultimately leads to an increase in ignorance and misguidance. The spread of ignorance is the first step to the spread of evils, which makes it obligatory upon the Muslims to work towards spreading knowledge and raising scholars who are among the necessary assets of any community.

10 Abu Dawud, *Sunan Abi Dawud*, Hadith No. 3641

Beware of Making Up Things About the Prophet

عَنِ المُغِيرَةِ رَضِيَ اللَّهُ عَنْهُ قَالَ سَمِعْتُ النَّبِيَّ صَلَّى اللهُ عَلَيْهِ
وَسَلَّمَ يَقُولُ إِنَّ كَذِبًا عَلَيَّ لَيْسَ كَكَذِبٍ عَلَى أَحَدٍ مَنْ كَذَبَ عَلَيَّ
مُتَعَمِّدًا ۞ فَلْيَتَبَوَّأْ مَقْعَدَهُ مِنَ النَّارِ

Al-Mughīrah ☙ reported: 'I heard the Prophet of Allah
☙ saying, "Lying about me is not the same as lying about
someone else. Whoever lies about me intentionally, then
let him take his seat in the Fire."'

Honesty and integrity are two indispensable characteristics for any
morally upright individual to uphold. When we inform another
person about something, we must ensure that the information we relay

is accurate and true. It is unworthy of any upright person to pass on information which they know is false and untrue. Everyone gets angry when they hear that someone has said something about them which is untrue. However, the sensitive nature of attributing something false to the Prophet Muhammad ﷺ is more significant than anything else. By now, you should know that the statements and teachings of the Prophet Muhammad ﷺ are referred to as hadith. His teachings are a form of revelation just as the Qur'an is a revelation, and both must be followed. In many places in the Qur'an, Allah commands Muslims to adhere to the Prophet's instructions. He says: *'And obey Allah and the Messenger, so that you may be shown mercy'* (*Āl 'Imrān* 3: 132). In another verse He says: *'If you dispute regarding a matter, then refer it back to Allah and the Messenger if you truly believe in Allah and the Final Day'* (*al-Nisā'* 4: 59). These are just a few of the verses which show the obligation of following the Messenger of Allah ﷺ.

The high status of prophetic statements is clear because the Sunnah is an explanation of the Qur'an and a clarification of it. The sayings of the Prophet Muhammad ﷺ are therefore powerful in terms of their explaining Islam. This hadith serves as a warning to anyone tempted to fabricate statements about the Prophet Muhammad ﷺ and claim that he said or did something he did not.

In spite of this hadith, there have been people, and there still are, who falsely attribute statements to the Prophet Muhammad ﷺ. Some do this intentionally, while others do it unintentionally (for instance, by sharing a fabricated hadith with people before verifying its authenticity). Those who do so are committing a grave sin, and this is quite clear from the hadith above: 'He who lies about me intentionally, then let him assume his place in the Fire.' Those who do it unintentionally are still blameworthy if they did not put enough effort into verifying statements that are attributed to the Prophet Muhammad ﷺ. As the statements of the Prophet Muhammad ﷺ are a source of guidance for mankind, spreading fabricated ahadith which he did not say causes an imbalance in the way people understand the Sunnah. It also causes people to act in incorrect ways because the condition of good action is that it is built upon correct knowledge.

This hadith teaches us that it is necessary upon Muslims to verify statements that reach them, especially those that are attributed to the Prophet ﷺ, whether they come through messages or through social media platforms or any other means. Such measures are taken to ensure that the Sunnah is taught in its purest form and that it is not clouded by false and inauthentic reports. The message in this hadith is not merely a recommendation, but a strict command by the Prophet Muhammad ﷺ to ensure that we only report true things about him.

23

The Importance of Monotheism

عن أَنَسَ بْنَ مَالِكٍ قَالَ ذُكِرَ لِي أَنَّ النَّبِيَّ صَلَّى اللهُ عَلَيْهِ وَسَلَّمَ قَالَ لِمُعَاذِ بْنِ جَبَلٍ مَنْ لَقِيَ اللَّهَ لاَ يُشْرِكُ بِهِ شَيْئًا دَخَلَ الجَنَّةَ قَالَ أَلاَ أُبَشِّرُ النَّاسَ قَالَ لاَ إِنِّي أَخَافُ أَنْ يَتَّكِلُوا

Anas ﷺ reported: 'I was informed that the Prophet ﷺ said to Mu'ādh ibn Jabal: "Whosoever will meet Allah without associating anything in worship with Him will go to Paradise." Mu'ādh asked the Prophet ﷺ: "Should I not inform the people of this good news?" The Prophet ﷺ replied: "No, I am afraid, lest they should (totally) depend upon it."'

The main message of Islam is the message of monotheism. That is to say that there is no god or deity and none is worthy of worship other than Allah. Monotheism is the heart of Islam; the fundamental and indispensable message Allah commanded His Messenger, the Prophet Muhammad ﷺ to convey to humankind. Human relationship with Allah has to start from the point of acknowledging His Oneness (*tawḥīd*). Polytheism, the opposite of monotheism, is the greatest offence one can commit. Allah is willing to forgive all sins, all crimes, all offences, but He does not forgive polytheism (*shirk*). This means that if a person dies committing *shirk* and has not repented for that sin, then Allah will not forgive them.

Shirk is the act of ascribing partners to Allah and it is considered one of the major sins. Islam is the religion of all the Prophets that have been sent by God, starting from the first man, Adam ﷺ down to the last and final Prophet, Prophet Muhammad ﷺ. Their religion is one. The Prophet Muhammad ﷺ said, 'The Prophets are paternal brothers; their mothers are different, but their religion is one.'[11] There may have been some variations in the method, style and manner of the acts of worshipping Allah (such as prayer, fasting, and other rulings), but the foundations of Islam in belief and character are the same for all the Prophets. The basis of the call of all the Prophets is to call people to the worship of God alone and to abandon the worship, in all its forms, of anyone other than Allah. Every Messenger that was sent by Allah would first begin by calling people to worship God alone (*tawḥīd*) and warn them against falling into *shirk*.

The reason why this is such an important issue is because it is connected to the purpose of our creation. Allah created us to obey Him. He says in the Qur'an: *'And I have not created the jinn and mankind except that they worship Me'* (*al-Dhāriyāt* 51: 56).

In this hadith the Prophet Muhammad ﷺ told Muʿādh ﷺ not to tell others of what he told him, for the fear that people may become complacent and forsake performing good deeds and simply rely on their belief in Allah alone to take them to Paradise. To do this would

11 Al-Bukhārī, *Ṣaḥīḥ al-Bukhārī*, Hadith No. 3443

be incorrect, because if we leave out good actions, the heart will end up becoming weaker until we are at risk of having our faith taken away from us and this is considered one of the biggest heartbreaks. To become distant from Allah is the most regrettable step any Muslim can take. It hardens the heart, diverts His guidance and causes a downward spiral of depression and sadness.

This hadith teaches Muslims the importance of monotheism, the belief in One God. It teaches us that it is the most important aspect for our salvation with Allah, Most High. The hadith also demonstrates that not everything we know must necessarily be shared with others. We should first consider who we are speaking to and based on that, decide whether it is appropriate to pass on certain types of knowledge to them or not. It is for this reason that Muʿādh ﷺ kept this hadith a secret until the end of his life. When he decided to narrate it to others, it was only because he feared passing away while having kept beneficial knowledge away from people.

Being Considerate

عَنْ أَبِى هُرَيْرَةَ أَنَّ رَسُولَ اللَّهِ صَلَّى اللهُ عَلَيْهِ وَسَلَّمَ قَالَ إِذَا صَلَّى
أَحَدُكُمْ لِلنَّاسِ فَلْيُخَفِّفْ فَإِنَّ مِنْهُمُ الضَّعِيفَ وَالسَّقِيمَ وَالكَبِيرَ
وَإِذَا صَلَّى أَحَدُكُمْ لِنَفْسِهِ فَلْيُطَوِّلْ مَا شَاءَ

Abū Hurayrah ❀ narrated that the Messenger of Allah
❀ said: 'If anyone of you leads the people in the prayer, he
should be light, for amongst them are the weak, the sick
and the old; and if one prays alone then he may prolong
(the prayer) as much as he wishes.'

Allah states in the Qur'an: *'Allah wishes to reduce the burden on you,
and man was created weak'* (al-Nisā' 4: 28). Allah never wants
to burden a soul with more than what it could bear. His principle
of ordering humankind to do something is based on the principle of
ease. Ease, or *'yusr'* in Arabic, is one of the key underlying features

of Islamic law so much so that the Prophet Muhammad ﷺ directly commanded Muslims to facilitate ease and to not make things difficult: 'Make things easy and do not make them difficult.'[12] In fact, although his own worship of Allah was of the highest standard—which included performing long prayers at night, fasting extra days more than anyone else, and much more—yet, when other people were involved, he never overburdened them; instead, he showed an excess amount of gentleness towards them.

On one occasion, the illustrious Companion Muʿādh ibn Jabal ؓ was leading the prayer and prolonged it. One of the men who were with him left the congregation and continued the prayer by himself, because he felt that Muʿādh ؓ was taking too long. The man complained about this to the Prophet Muhammad ﷺ who became extremely angry and said to Muʿādh ؓ, 'Are you seeking to cause *fitnah* (trouble), O Muʿādh?' He continued: 'If one of you leads the prayer, then let him keep it light, because behind him are the elderly, and the weak, and those who have needs. While if one of you prays alone, then he may prolong it as he wishes.' This does not mean that the imam should speed through the prayers, but only that he should keep it light. This was something that the Prophet Muhammad ﷺ perfected. Anas ibn Mālik ؓ said, 'I have never seen anyone more complete in his prayer and more concise in his prayer, than the Messenger of Allah ﷺ.'

Islam teaches us to be balanced in all areas of life and not just in our prayers. Anyone who takes on a role of leadership or authority should be gentle to those under their responsibility and be wary of being difficult. A very important lesson this hadith teaches us is to be considerate towards others. Not everyone is the same, with the same ability and same circumstances. It is important that we behave considerately towards others lest we put them off Islam or worshipping Allah or cause them hardship.

---

12 Al-Bukhārī, *Ṣaḥīḥ al-Bukhārī*, Hadith No. 6125

25

Honesty in Buying and Selling

عن حَكِيمَ بْنَ حِزَامٍ ﵁ عَنِ النَّبِيِّ ﷺ قَالَ الْبَيِّعَانِ بِالْخِيَارِ مَا لَمْ يَتَفَرَّقَا فَإِنْ صَدَقَا وَبَيَّنَا بُورِكَ لَهُمَا فِي بَيْعِهِمَا وَإِنْ كَذَبَا وَكَتَمَا مُحِقَتْ بَرَكَةُ بَيْعِهِمَا

Ḥakīm ibn Ḥizām ﵁ narrated that the Prophet ﷺ said: 'The buyer and the seller have the option of cancelling or confirming the sale unless they separate. If they spoke the truth and made clear the defects of the goods, then they would be blessed in their bargain, and if they told lies and hid some facts, their bargain would be deprived of Allah's blessings.'

The beauty of Islam includes the fact that it has taught us how to behave in all areas of life. Money and wealth are commonly spoken about subjects in the Qur'an and Sunnah, due to their great importance. In fact, the preservation of wealth is one of the five objectives (*maqāṣid al-sharīʿah*) that Islam has come to protect. It does this through the prohibition of taking what one has no right to take and through encouraging honesty when dealing with money and property.

This hadith mentions one of the golden principles that teaches us how we should approach buying, selling and wealth. The first part dictates that we should be easy-going with whom we trade, rather than being rash and aggressive. This is emphasised in another hadith in which the Prophet Muhammad ﷺ said, 'May Allah have mercy upon the one who is easy when buying, easy when selling and easy when lending.'[13]

The hadith reported by Ḥakīm ibn Ḥizām ؓ teaches Muslims that Allah's blessings descend upon the one who is honest when dealing with money. A person may earn money in dishonest ways but will never feel the true benefit and blessing of that money unless they remain truthful. The amount of earnings that a person shall make has already been decreed before he or she is even born. Therefore, even if we attempt to earn money through unlawful means, we can be certain that we will not earn a penny more than what Allah had decreed for us.

Therefore, we should be clear about what we are buying; we must not cheat or hide defects in things we wish to sell; and we must ensure to give people the amount that is due to them, without deceiving them in any way. Doing otherwise would be a cause of removing Allah's blessings from our property.

---

13 Al-Bukhārī, *Ṣaḥīḥ al-Bukhārī*, Hadith No. 1368

26

The Virtues of Surah al-Baqarah

عَنْ أَبِي مَسْعُودٍ رَضِيَ اللَّهُ عَنْهُ قَالَ قَالَ النَّبِيُّ صَلَّى اللهُ عَلَيْهِ
وَسَلَّمَ مَنْ قَرَأَ بِالْآيَتَيْنِ مِنْ آخِرِ سُورَةِ البَقَرَةِ فِي لَيْلَةٍ كَفَتَاهُ

Abū Masʿūd ﷺ narrated that the Prophet ﷺ said: 'If somebody recited the last two verses of *Surah al-Baqarah* at night, that will be sufficient for him.'

The Qur'an is the ultimate source of guidance for mankind in this life. Qur'anic guidance can be understood in both the physical sense, as well as the spiritual. The spiritual guidance makes up the main dimension of the Qur'anic message. The Qur'an calls humankind to the worship of Allah alone, belief in the Unseen, perfection of righteous actions and character. Along with the spiritual guidance, the Qur'an provides physical guidance in the sense of providing protection from harm from the physical and metaphysical world. Indeed, the Qur'an is a blessing and guidance in every way. One of the ways in which it is a blessing is that it is a cure and protection from evil and other types of harm.

In this hadith, the Prophet Muhammad ﷺ wanted to encourage us to recite the last two verses (285 and 286) of *al-Baqarah*, the second chapter of the Qur'an, at night. These verses can be recited at any time during the night, and one does not necessarily have to wait until they are in bed to recite them.

The virtue of reciting these two verses is that it will provide us with protection from evil. This is what is meant by the Prophet's words, '...that will be sufficient for him'. In fact, it has been interpreted by scholars in several ways, the most prominent of those interpretations being two: firstly, it suffices a person from performing the night prayer; or secondly, it suffices a person as a protection from *jinn* or any other harm that may befall them. Since the mercy of Allah is vast, there is no reason why it cannot encompass both those things.

These two verses recited are a protection and a form of shield, just as the Prophet Muhammad ﷺ taught us that reciting the *Āyat al-Kursī* each night grants a person protection and they shall not have any Satanic force come near them that night. This is because evil and harm can come in many different forms, including harms from the world of the Unseen, such as magic, *jinn*, and the evil eye, all of which are potentially harmful as we are taught in the Qur'an and Hadith. Since these types of harms cannot be physically seen or easily anticipated, the Prophet Muhammad ﷺ guided us towards methods of protection from such things. However, as pre-requisite, we must first have total faith in Allah's power to protect us. Allah says in the Qur'an regarding magic: *'And they shall not harm with it [magic] anyone except with God's permission'* (*al-Baqarah* 2: 102).

This hadith also shows us that protection from these things does not require extreme forms of *ruqyah* and treatments, such as beating, screaming, and excessive reading. It is sufficient to recite *Surah al-Fātiḥah*, a few verses from *Surah al-Baqarah*, and the last two chapters of the Qur'an. These are all recommended things to recite as a form of *ruqyah* and protection, and it is not correct to go to extremes with *ruqyha*, because the Prophetic *ruqyah* has always been simple. However, once again, these verses should be recited with certainty that the Qur'an is a cure for all evil and that Allah is able to do all things.

27

Atonement for Believers

عن عَائِشَةَ رَضِيَ اللَّهُ عَنْهَا زَوْجَ النَّبِيِّ صَلَّى اللهُ عَلَيْهِ وَسَلَّمَ قَالَتْ قَالَ رَسُولُ اللَّهِ صَلَّى اللهُ عَلَيْهِ وَسَلَّمَ مَا مِنْ مُصِيبَةٍ تُصِيبُ الْمُسْلِمَ إِلَّا كَفَّرَ اللَّهُ بِهَا عَنْهُ حَتَّى الشَّوْكَةِ يُشَاكُهَا

'Ā'ishah ﷺ reported that the Messenger of Allah ﷺ said: 'No calamity befalls a Muslim except that Allah expiates some of his sins because of it, even if it were just a prick he receives from a thorn.'

Allah did not create this world as Paradise for everyone. His wisdom dictates that this life would be filled with trials and challenges of all sorts. This is something that Allah has promised in the Qur'an: *'We will surely test you with something of fear, hunger, loss of wealth and lives and fruits, but give good tidings to the patient; those who, when disaster strikes them, say, "We belong to Allah, and to Him we will return"'* (*al-Baqarah* 2: 155). Even those closest to Allah, such as the Prophets, faced great trials in their lives. The Qur'an is filled with examples of the challenges the previous Prophets and the Prophet Muhammad ﷺ faced, so that we can take them as role models and so that we realise that difficulties are a part of life. It is these difficulties that take us closer to Allah, making us realise that He is the One who does not disappoint us. When we establish this understanding, we can truly aspire to be the best of believers.

The reason why Allah has made life on earth so challenging is to test us, to see who amongst us is the best in good deeds and obedient to Allah in the face of hardship and difficulties. Allah says in the Qur'an: *'Do people think that they would be left only to say, "We believe," without being put to test? Indeed, we have tested those who were before them, so Allah will surely know the ones who are truthful, and He will surely know the liars"* (*al-'Ankabūt* 29: 2).

Allah describes Himself as Most Forgiving (al-Ghafūr), Most Loving (al-Wadūd), Most Merciful (al-Raḥmān), and Most Kind (al-Raḥīm). Allah is the Most Forgiving and He loves to forgive. He knows best that humans are weak, and that they will err repeatedly. For this, Allah has made opportunities for people to seek His pardon and to repent. One of the most beautiful ways Allah has devised to forgive us is through the daily problems we endure. Allah's mercy upon us means that none of these challenges and hardships are in vain. If we react in the way that we have been taught to react to calamities and struggles, then our reward will be great in the next life, and we shall live a life of contentment in this life, knowing that everything that happens only happens with the decree of Allah. This is to the extent that even the slightest of discomfort will not go unnoticed. Allah will compensate us for anything that happens to us in this life, no matter how big or small, and this should always be remembered whenever we face any type of harm, sadness, distress, or pain. Whenever we face any calamity, we should say, *'innā lillāhi wa innā ilayhi rāji'ūn'* (Indeed we belong to Allah and verily to Him is our return).

28

Always have a Good Opinion of Other Muslims

عَنْ أَبِي هُرَيْرَةَ قَالَ قَالَ رَسُولُ اللَّهِ صَلَّى اللهُ عَلَيْهِ وَسَلَّمَ إِيَّاكُمْ
وَالظَّنَّ فَإِنَّ الظَّنَّ أَكْذَبُ الحَدِيثِ وَلاَ تَحَسَّسُوا وَلاَ تَجَسَّسُوا
وَلاَ تَبَاغَضُوا وَلاَ تَدَابَرُوا وَكُونُوا عِبَادَ اللَّهِ إِخْوَانًا

Abū Hurayrah رضي الله عنه narrated that the Messenger of Allah ﷺ said: 'Beware of suspicion, for it is the worst of false tales and do not look for the other's faults and do not spy and do not hate each other, and do not forsake (cut your relations with) one another, and O Allah's servants, be brothers!'

Unity and cohesion in the community are one of the greatest objectives in Islam. Allah says in the Qur'an: *'And hold firmly to the rope of Allah altogether and do not become divided. And remember the favour of Allah upon you - when you were enemies and He brought your hearts together and you became, by His favour, brothers'* (*Āl 'Imrān* 3: 103).

The Qur'an and the Prophet Muhammad ﷺ have warned us sternly against anything that causes disunity and dispute. The first step to disunity and enmity is distrust. The moment there is no trust between people, whether husband and wife, siblings, family members, or Muslims in general, then problems will inevitably arise, and perhaps become quite severe. This is why we have been commanded to think well of one another and to assume the best in others. Allah says in the Qur'an: *'O you who believe, avoid many suspicions, for some of suspicion is sinful; and do not spy on one another, nor backbite one another'* (*al-Ḥujurāt* 49: 12). This verse of *Surah al-Ḥujurāt* indicates that distrust often leads to suspicion, and then to spying on one another to seek out their faults, which then often leads to backbiting. These things then result in the other harms mentioned in the hadith, such as deserting our friends and family and spreading hatred amongst each other. This is why the root cause of all of this, which is suspicion, has been prohibited in the Qur'an and in this hadith. As long as there is a probable justification for the words or actions of another person, we should do our best to assume that they have a valid excuse, as opposed to assuming the worst. We would wish others to assume the best in us, so we should be the same towards others.

Finally, let us not forget that Satan wants to create hatred and enmity amongst us. If he can divide us then he has achieved one of his greatest goals. So, let us remember that being suspicious plays into the hands of Satan; it does not please Allah, but it makes Satan very happy. Therefore, as Muslims, we should do our best to not fall into Satan's trap or it would lead to a bigger downfall in our lives.

29

Keeping Sins a Secret

عن أبى هُرَيْرَةَ قال سَمِعْتُ رَسُولَ اللَّهِ صَلَّى اللهُ عَلَيْهِ وَسَلَّمَ
يَقُولُ كُلُّ أُمَّتِي مُعَافًى إِلَّا المُجَاهِرِينَ وَإِنَّ مِنَ المُجَاهَرَةِ أَنْ يَعْمَلَ
الرَّجُلُ بِاللَّيْلِ عَمَلًا ثُمَّ يُصْبِحَ وَقَدْ سَتَرَهُ اللّٰه عَلَيْهِ فَيَقُولَ يَا
فُلَانُ عَمِلْتُ البَارِحَةَ كَذَا وَكَذَا وَقَدْ بَاتَ يَسْتُرُهُ رَبُّهُ ۞ وَيُصْبِحُ
يَكْشِفُ سِتْرَ اللَّهِ عَنْه

Abū Hurayrah ﵁ narrated: 'I heard the Messenger of Allah ﷺ saying: "All the sins of my followers will be forgiven except those of the *Mujāhirīn* (those who sin openly or disclose their sins to the people). An example of such negligence is that a person commits a sin at night and though Allah screens it from the public, he comes in the morning, and says, 'O so-and-so, I did such-and-such (evil) deed yesterday,' though he spent his night screened by his Lord (none knowing about his sin) and in the morning he removes Allah's screen from himself.'"

Allah Almighty has told us that humans were created weak: *'And man was created weak'* (*al-Nisā'* 4: 28). That weakness exists in our bodies, our intellect, our emotions, and also in our desire to commit sins. It is reported that Prophet Muhammad ﷺ said, 'Every one of the children of Adam sins, and the best of those who sin are those who constantly repent [to Allah].' This shows that it is normal for a person to fall into sin and to make errors. This is part of the nature of humans. However, the Qur'an has guided us towards how to act when we fall into sin. Only through continuous *istighfār* (repentance) and a firm commitment not to repeat the sin, can we be forgiven by Almighty Allah.

One of the things that has been emphasised whenever we fall into sin is that we should keep them private and conceal them from others. Private sins are lighter than public sins, because when sins become public, they become more normalised, which results in the spread of evil in the community. Allah says in the Qur'an: *'Surely, those who like that lewdness spreads among the believers, for them there is painful punishment in this world and the hereafter'* (*al-Nūr* 24: 19).

The hadith also teaches us that exposing our sins is a lack of gratitude to Allah who blessed us by concealing our sins for us and protecting us. Rather than being grateful and turning to Him in regret and repentance, a person instead exposes their sins to others. If this exposure of sin is done to boast about the sinful act, then that is surely a major sin. However, even if it was not done with that intention, sharing one's sins with others remains prohibited in Islam. On the Day of Judgment, Allah will remind us of every sin we committed. If we covered them in this life, then we can be hopeful that Allah will forgive them and excuse us for them in the Hereafter. However, if we were to carelessly reveal those sins when Allah has covered them, then we can blame only ourselves.

It should be noted that covering our sins up is not a type of hypocrisy as some people may believe. Rather, it is something that Allah has commanded us to do. We may fall into error and admit to our weakness, but when we choose to hide them from others, it shows that our hearts are still alive and that deep down, we recognise that we have made a mistake. Private sins are nonetheless dangerous if they are constantly committed, because they can damage us spiritually. Ultimately, whether we commit sins in private or in public, by mistake or on purpose, we must always turn to Allah in repentance.

30

Making Up With the Person you have Fallen Out With

عَنْ أَبِي أَيُّوبَ الأَنْصَارِيِّ أَنَّ رَسُولَ اللَّهِ صَلَّى اللهُ عَلَيْهِ وَسَلَّمَ قَالَ لاَ يَحِلُّ لِرَجُلٍ أَنْ يَهْجُرَ أَخَاهُ فَوْقَ ثَلاَثِ لَيَالٍ يَلْتَقِيَانِ فَيُعْرِضُ هَذَا وَيُعْرِضُ هَذَا وَخَيْرُهُمَا الَّذِى يَبْدَأُ بِالسَّلاَمِ

Abū Ayyūb Al-Anṣārī ﷺ narrated that the Messenger of Allah ﷺ said: 'It is not lawful for a man to desert his brother for more than three nights. (Such that) when they meet, one of them turns his face away from the other, and the other turns his face from the former; and the better of the two is the one who greets the other first.'

In a previous hadith, we discussed the importance of brotherhood/sisterhood and the need for unity and togetherness. This hadith is also a part of that discussion and emphasises the importance of unity. Humans are social beings that constantly interact with one another. However, our natural differences mean that we also differ in our views, our preferences, and what we feel is best. This can sometimes lead to arguments that can get out of hand if they are not kept under control. Disagreeing and even having disputes with others is something that we will inevitably experience several times in life. In fact, even the greatest of people argued, such as Prophet Mūsā ﷺ and his brother, Prophet Hārūn ﷺ, as mentioned in the Qur'an. It is therefore normal to expect arguments and disagreements to crop up every now and then.

However, arguments can become excessive and damaging. In order to address this issue the Prophet Muhammad ﷺ gave a limit of three days to allow people to cool down before they need to put effort into resolving their issues and differences. After three days, if the two people who are in disagreement meet each other, then the least required from them is to greet each other, and the best of the two is the one who gives the greetings of *salām* first. This is especially important when disputes arise between family members, because cutting off ties with family is an even greater sin than deserting any other Muslim. This rule also applies to husband and wife. Spouses usually fall into dispute, but to not speak to each other for more than three nights is sinful, and the one who initiates some effort to resolve such a dispute will be rewarded, because Allah says in the Qur'an: *'And resolving [disputes] is better'* (*al-Nisā'* 4: 128).

31

Attaining Islamic Knowledge

قَالَ النَّبِيِّ ﷺ قَالَ وَعَنْ مُعَاوِيَةَ
من يرد الله به خيرا يفقهه فى الدين

Muʿāwiyah ﷺ said, 'I heard the Prophet ﷺ saying: "If Allah wants good for a person, He makes him comprehend the religion."'

Learning and acquiring knowledge is mandatory for all Muslims. Islam encourages everyone to acquire more than its essential articles. Islam has honoured those who possess knowledge and holds them at an elevated position. In the Qur'an, Allah tells us that those who have knowledge are superior to those who do not have knowledge. *"Say, are they equal, those who have knowledge and those who do not?"* (*al-Zumar* 39: 9).

This hadith is one of the most important Prophetic traditions that talks about the topic of Islamic knowledge. It shows that the one who has a good understanding of the Qur'an, the teachings of the Prophet

Muhammad ﷺ, and how to act according to Islamic teachings has been given a great gift by Allah.

There are many reasons why knowledge is considered to be such a great thing. Here are three main reasons:

Firstly, we will not be able to act in the correct way, unless we first have the right understanding of the correct way. Knowledge comes before action, otherwise our actions may end up being wrong. Having knowledge therefore helps us make correct decisions in our day-to-day life and it helps us reduce the mistakes we may make.

Secondly, knowledge is not something that is restricted to the one who learns it. Acts of worship such as prayers and fasts, although important acts of worship, are usually only beneficial for the person themself. On the other hand, knowledge can be shared with others, which means that many others can also benefit from the knowledge that we possess.

Finally, knowledge teaches us about our Creator and the best ways to worship Him. There are specific ways for us to worship Allah and we cannot simply worship Allah in any way we like. That's why Allah has sent Messengers to show us the right way to worship Him. Through learning, we can follow the religion that Allah has sent, and practise it in a way that is pleasing to Him.

It should also be noted that this hadith includes the goodness of this life and the next. This means that the one who has acquired beneficial knowledge and acts upon it will not only be rewarded greatly in the Hereafter, but will also see many benefits in this life. From those benefits is that a person of knowledge will be able to help people solve their problems. Muslims are always in need of great scholars, both male and female, who understand the religion correctly, so that they can contribute in guiding the community towards doing good and towards keeping away from evil.

32

Maintaining Balance in Worshipping Allah

عَنْ أَبِي هُرَيْرَةَ عَنِ النَّبِيِّ ﷺ قَالَ إِنَّ الدِّينَ يُسْرٌ وَلَنْ يُشَادَّ الدِّينَ أَحَدٌ إِلاَّ غَلَبَهُ فَسَدِّدُوا وَقَارِبُوا وَأَبْشِرُوا وَاسْتَعِينُوا بِالْغَدْوَةِ وَالرَّوْحَةِ وَشَىْءٍ مِنَ الدُّلْجَةِ

Abū Hurayrah ؓ narrated that the Prophet ﷺ said: 'Religion is easy and whoever overburdens himself in his religion will not be able to continue in that way. So you should not be extreme, but try to be near to perfection and receive the good tidings that you will be rewarded; and gain strength by worshipping in the mornings, the afternoons, and during the last hours of the nights.'

It is part of our human nature to prefer ease over hardship. If there are different ways to get something done, we would normally choose the easiest way possible. This is not only part of nature, but it is also something that Allah wants for us. Allah says in the Qur'an: *'Allah wants ease for you, and He does not want hardship for you'* (*al-Baqarah* 2: 185). 'Ā'ishah ﵂ said, 'Whenever the Messenger of Allah ﷺ was given a choice between two things, he would always choose the easier of them, as long as it did not involve sin.' The objective of Islam is not to make life difficult, but to help people achieve spiritual purification with ease. The Prophet Muhammad ﷺ came with a message to reduce the burden upon us, as Allah tells us in the Qur'an: *'Allah wishes to lessen the burden upon you, and man was created weak'* (*al-Nisā'* 4: 28). The Companions loved Islam and the Prophet ﷺ. Islam provided for them liberation from idolatry and falsehood and introduced them to Allah. It gave them the realisation of worshipping Allah properly, and what awaits them in return for their faith and deeds. Sometimes, this deep love for Allah and eagerness to get closer to Him made them overburden themselves with acts of worship. So, the Prophet Muhammad ﷺ had to regularly remind them that the religion of Islam is ease and that it is not correct to be excessive in it. Rather, we should do that which we are capable of doing consistently without overburdening ourselves or others, and without neglecting others' rights, such as those of our parents, relatives and the community in general.

The story of 'Abdullāh ibn 'Amr ibn al-'Āṣ ﵁ is an excellent example. He used to fast and recite the whole Qur'an every single day. The Prophet Muhammad ﷺ suggested to him to fast three days a month and to complete the recitation of the Qur'an each month. But 'Abdullāh ﵁ wanted to do more, so eventually he was given permission to fast every other day and to recite the complete Qur'an once a week.[14] However, when he got older, he regretted not taking the initial advice of the Prophet Muhammad ﷺ because he found that it was difficult to keep up with these many acts of worship consistently. This means that it is better to consistently perform good deeds in small amounts than to

14 See: Al-Bukhārī, *Ṣaḥīḥ al-Bukhārī*, Hadith No. 4767

perform a lot inconsistently.

This hadith teaches us to avoid being extreme in our practice of Islam. The optimal way of worshipping Allah is in moderation and that was the way the Prophet Muhammad ﷺ used to do it. Being extreme in anything is discouraged whereas being moderate is the way of the Muslim. It is worth noting that in the advice the Prophet ﷺ gave to ʿAbdullāh ibn ʿAmr ibn al-ʿĀṣ, he also stated that Allah will not get tired of giving us spiritual reward, but we will get tired of worshipping Allah. Therefore, we should be consistent and moderate in what we do throughout our lives in order to create a balance in worshipping Allah.

At the same time, it is also important to remember that we should never label someone as an 'extremist' just because they perform more acts of worship than an average Muslim. As we increase in spirituality, we crave to be in the remembrance and worship of Allah as much as we can. As long as we are not overburdening ourselves or our loved ones and dependents in the process, as long as we get sufficient nourishment, rest and good company, there is no harm in setting higher goals in terms of spirituality.

33

Paying off your Debts

عَنْ سَلَمَةَ بْنِ الأَكْوَعِ رَضِيَ اللَّهُ عَنْهُ أَنَّ النَّبِيَّ صَلَّى اللهُ عَلَيْهِ وَسَلَّمَ أُتِيَ بِجَنَازَةٍ لِيُصَلِّيَ عَلَيْهَا فَقَالَ هَلْ عَلَيْهِ مِنْ دَيْنٍ؟ قَالُوا لَا، فَصَلَّى عَلَيْهِ ثُمَّ أُتِيَ بِجَنَازَةٍ أُخْرَى فَقَالَ هَلْ عَلَيْهِ مِنْ دَيْنٍ؟ قَالُوا نَعَمْ، قَالَ صَلُّوا عَلَى صَاحِبِكُمْ قَالَ أَبُو قَتَادَةَ عَلَيَّ دَيْنُهُ يَا رَسُولَ اللَّهِ، فَصَلَّى عَلَيْهِ

Salamah ibn al-Akwaʿ ﷺ narrated: 'A dead person was brought to the Prophet ﷺ so that he might lead the funeral prayer for him. He asked, "Is he in debt?" When the people replied in the negative, he led the funeral prayer. Another dead person was brought, and he asked, "Is he in debt?" They said, "Yes." He (refused to lead the prayer and) said, "Lead the prayer of your friend." Abu Qatādah said, "O Messenger of Allah! I undertake to pay his debt." Allah's Messenger ﷺ then led his funeral prayer.'

Islam has taught us to minimise our reliance upon others and instead work to provide for ourselves. At the same time, life is hardly easy and from time to time we all need financial help from others in order to improve our situation. If there is no real need, then it is discouraged and offensive to borrow money from other people or institutions. Taking loans can make a person vulnerable and weak because there is always the uncertainty of it not being paid back. The Prophet Muhammad ﷺ would seek refuge from debt so much so that it was once said to the Messenger of Allah ﷺ, 'O Messenger of Allah, you seek refuge in Allah from debt so much.' He replied, 'If a person falls into debt, he lies when he speaks, and he breaks promises.' This is because the one in debt may not be able to return what he owes on time, which could lead him to lying and making up excuses. It can also be humiliating for a person, since the one who lent the money may feel like he is in control of the borrower because of the latter's indebtedness. These are some of the harms which come out of being in debt. This is why the Prophet Muhammad ﷺ would so regularly ask Allah to protect him from debt. Owing someone money is a serious matter. In some cases, it can break family ties and destroy friendships. The Prophet Muhammad ﷺ wanted to make the seriousness of debt clear to his followers and did not want people to become negligent and lenient with taking loans. To teach his followers the seriousness of this matter, he refused to pray the funeral prayer over a Muslim who passed away and had unpaid debts. Although the Prophet ﷺ did give permission to take loans for those who have a genuine need, we should rush to pay off all debts as early as possible. This hadith teaches us to be extra cautious in taking loans and to repay them as soon as possible. Nowadays, since we live in the age of credit cards and loan payments, it's crucial that we remember this valuable teaching of Islam.

34

The Reward of Illness and Journey

قَالَ أَبُو بُرْدَةَ سَمِعْتُ أَبَا مُوسَى مِرَارًا يَقُولُ قَالَ رَسُولُ اللَّهِ صَلَّى اللهُ عَلَيْهِ وَسَلَّمَ إِذَا مَرِضَ العَبْدُ أَوْ سَافَرَ كُتِبَ لَهُ مِثْلُ مَا كَانَ يَعْمَلُ مُقِيمًا صَحِيحًا

Abū Burdah ﵁ said, 'I heard Abū Mūsā saying several times that the Messenger of Allah ﷺ said: "When a slave falls ill or travels, then he will get a reward similar to what he gets for good deeds practiced at home and in good health."'

Illness and travel are part and parcel of life and everyone at some point in their lives will experience these to some extent. It is from Allah's mercy upon us that He does not hold us to account for those things that are beyond our control and ability. We are accountable for the effort that we put in. As long as a person has done the best they can and as sincerely as possible, then Allah has promised that their deeds will not go to waste. Allah says in the Qur'an: *"Those who have believed and done righteous deeds, We will not allow to go to waste the reward of those who do good"* (*al-Kahf* 18: 30).

This hadith teaches us that we will be rewarded according to our intentions. If we want to do good deeds, but something out of our control stopped us from doing so, then we will not miss out on the reward in any way. For example, if someone usually fasts on Mondays, but falls ill on a Monday and is consequently unable to fast, he or she will, nevertheless, be rewarded as though that fast was completed, because what happened was beyond their control. Similarly, if someone missed the prayer in the mosque because they had to look after a sick relative, their reward will not be decreased, and they will be rewarded in the same fashion. The same applies to a person who was prevented from good deeds due to travel.

Some scholars of Hadith have said that another example of the application of this hadith, is calling others to Islam or towards doing good deeds. They may accept what we say, or they may reject it. Either way, we are rewarded by Allah. This is also why all the Prophets of Allah are considered to be successful in carrying out their prophetic task. Although many of their people rejected their call to worship Allah, the Prophets carried out their duty of calling others to Allah sincerely. What is beyond their control is no fault of theirs.

Imam Aḥmad ibn Ḥanbal advised his son to always practise harbouring good intentions and the love of doing good, because even if we are not able to achieve what we intended, our intention alone would not allow us to miss out on the rewards of the deed.

35

You will be with Those Whom you Love

عن أنس رضى الله عنه أن رجلا سأل النبي ﷺ عن الساعة فقال متى الساعة؟ قال وماذا أعددت لها؟ قال لا شىء إلا أنى أحب الله ورسوله ﷺ فقال أنت مع من أحببت قال أنس فما فرحنا بشىء فزحنا بقول النبي ﷺ أنت مع من أحببت قال أنس فأنا أحب النبي ﷺ وأبا بكر وعمر وأرجو أن أكون معهم بحبي إياهم وإن لم عمل بمثل أعمالهم

Anas ؓ narrated: 'A man asked the Prophet ﷺ about the Hour (i.e., Day of Judgment) saying: "When will the Hour be?" The Prophet ﷺ said: "What have you prepared for it?" The man said: "Nothing, except that I love Allah and His Messenger ﷺ." The Prophet said: "You will be with those whom you love." We had never been as happy as we were on hearing the Prophet ﷺ saying, "You will be with those whom you love." And I love the Prophet ﷺ, Abu Bakr and 'Umar, and I hope that I will be with them because of my love for them, though my deeds are not similar to theirs.'

This great hadith has so many lessons for us to take into consideration. Firstly, it teaches us that if someone passes away, then their Day of Judgment has begun as far as they are concerned, because they no longer have the opportunity of performing any further good deeds, therefore their reckoning is imminent. Wasting time and being neglectful in this life will be a cause of great regret for us after our death. Allah refers to the Day of Judgment as the 'Day of Regret' in the Qur'an: *'And warn them of the Day of Regret'* (*Maryam* 19: 39).

This beautiful hadith also shows the exceptional character of the Prophet Muhammad ﷺ in the way he gives hope to people and makes them feel optimistic. He was not someone who made people lose hope in Allah. Loving Allah, His Messengers, and righteous people, particularly the Prophet's Companions, is something which can lead a person to Paradise, because it is proof that the individual loves good. This is because our love for the Prophet Muhammad ﷺ and his Companions is due to our love for Allah and due to the fact that Allah loves them. However, we will truly be able to love the Messenger ﷺ and his Companions, as well as the great scholars of Islam, only if we know who they are and learn about the great service they have done to teach and preserve Allah's religion. This will not only put great love in our hearts for them but also push us towards following in their footsteps. This hadith is also a warning against loving or being on the side of evildoers and oppressors. If your beloved and closest friends are people of corruption, sin and mischief then you risk being resurrected with them on the Day of Judgment. We should, therefore, surround ourselves with people of goodness and people who bring us closer to Allah, as this will have an impact on us in this life and the next.

The Three Qualities of Faith

عَنْ أَنَسِ بْنِ مَالِكٍ رَضِيَ اللَّهُ عَنْهُ عَنِ النَّبِيِّ صَلَّى اللهُ عَلَيْهِ
وَسَلَّمَ قَالَ ثَلاَثٌ مَنْ كُنَّ فِيهِ وَجَدَ حَلاَوَةَ الإِيمَانِ أَنْ يَكُونَ
اللَّهُ وَرَسُولُهُ أَحَبَّ إِلَيْهِ مِمَّا سِوَاهُمَا وَأَنْ يُحِبَّ الْمَرْءَ لاَ يُحِبُّهُ إِلَّا لِلَّهِ
وَأَنْ يَكْرَهَ أَنْ يَعُودَ فِي الْكُفْرِ كَمَا يَكْرَهُ أَنْ يُقْذَفَ فِي النَّارِ

Anas ibn Mālik ﷺ narrated that the Prophet ﷺ said: 'Whoever possesses the following three qualities will find the sweetness of faith: the one to whom Allah and His Apostle become dearer than anything else; one who loves a person only for Allah's sake; and one who hates to revert to disbelief as he hates to be thrown into the fire.'

The sweetness of faith is a blessing everyone should ask Allah to grant them. The one who finds this sweetness of faith will experience contentment in life, because regardless of the challenges that life throws at them, they know that Allah and the eternal life in the Hereafter are far greater. When someone loves Allah and His Messenger ﷺ more than anything else, they are never let down. Everything we love in this life is at risk of disappearing or changing. That is the nature of life. But the one thing that will always remain is our love for Allah. Love for Allah can be acquired only when He is in the centre of our hearts and through our continuous remembrance of Him.

In this hadith, the Prophet Muhammad ﷺ mentioned three qualities of a high level of faith. Firstly, loving Allah and His Messenger ﷺ over anything and everyone else—whether it is our parents, peers, teachers, society, and even our own heart and its desires. When we are able to put Allah and His Messenger ﷺ first and give them priority in our lives; when we can, at every juncture in life, stop and ask ourselves, 'Would Allah be pleased with this?'; when we learn to replace thoughts like 'What will my friends think of me if I didn't do such-and-such thing?' with 'What will my beloved Prophet ﷺ think of me if he were to see me do such-and-such thing?', only then will we begin to taste the sweetness of faith. When we truly love someone, we rush to do things that would make them pleased with us. Interestingly, that is also when following their orders and wishes would come to us easily, without any feeling of coercion.

Secondly, loving a person purely for the sake of Allah. This is the best and purest type of love because it seeks no worldly expectations or benefits. Love based only on mutual benefit or worldly desire does not last and may not always be sincere. However, when love is due to Allah's sake, it remains. This is because the reason we love the person is neither their status nor what they can or cannot do for us, rather it is the Pleasure of Allah and the rewards He has promised us—the only thing that is constant and worth striving for. Simply put, loving purely for the sake of Allah means that we love the person only because Allah wants us to love the person; any other reason for our love is only secondary.

It is worth mentioning that the love that exists between husband and wife, although naturally strong, should also contain a love for Allah's sake. This is because a person's spouse may change in their beauty or wealth or health, which may lead to reduced love for the spouse. However, when marital love is built upon pure love that is connected to Allah, then this calls for Allah's mercy and blessing to descend upon such a marriage, regardless of other worldly factors. This is why no pre-marital relationship can ever give us such blessings and rewards.

Finally, the third quality mentioned in the hadith is the dislike of disbelief. When a person feels indifferent to disbelief, then it is difficult for them to appreciate Allah's blessing upon them of guiding them to Islam. *'Praise to Allah who has guided us to this; and we would never have been guided if Allah had not guided us'* (*al-A'rāf* 7: 43).

We can see from this hadith that the sweetness of pure faith comes from loving Allah, loving those who love Allah, and loving the things that Allah loves. The key to attaining these qualities is to know Him and His Messenger ﷺ because it will naturally make us love what they love and dislike what they dislike.

Reliance on Allah

عن أَنَس قَالَ حَدَّثَنِي أَبُو بَكْرٍ رَضِيَ اللَّهُ عَنْهُ قَالَ كُنْتُ مَعَ النَّبِيِّ صَلَّى اللهُ عَلَيْهِ وَسَلَّمَ فِي الغَارِ فَرَأَيْتُ آثَارَ الْمُشْرِكِينَ قُلْتُ يَا رَسُولَ اللَّهِ لَوْ أَنَّ أَحَدَهُمْ رَفَعَ قَدَمَهُ رَآنَا قَالَ مَا ظَنُّكَ بِاثْنَيْنِ اللَّهُ ثَالِثُهُمَا

Anas ibn Mālik ﵁ related: 'Abu Bakr ﵁ told me: "I was in the company of the Prophet ﷺ in the cave, and on seeing the traces of the pagans, I said: 'O Messenger of Allah, if one of them (pagans) should lift up his foot, he will see us.' He replied: 'What do you think of two, the third of whom is Allah?'"'

As we saw in Hadith 16 of this book, the closest and most beloved of the Companions to the Prophet Muhammad ﷺ were 'Ā'ishah among the women, and her father Abu Bakr and Umar among the men.

Abu Bakr would accompany the Prophet at all times, and all the Companions knew him to be the closest person to the Messenger of Allah. This hadith captures an incident that took place during the *hijrah* (migration) of the Prophet when Abu Bakr was given the honour of accompanying him. On their way to Madinah, the disbelievers of Quraysh were after them. At one point, when the Quraysh men were very close to the cave they were hiding out in, Abu Bakr feared that they would be easily spotted. The Prophet Muhammad assured Abu Bakr and reminded him that Allah was on their side, so there was nothing to worry about. The Qur'an also mentions this incident:

'If you do not aid the Prophet – then Allah has already aided him when those who disbelieved had driven him out (of Makkah), and he was one of two, when they were in the cave and he said to his companion, "Do not grieve; indeed, Allah is with us." So, Allah sent down His tranquillity upon him and supported him with troops that you did not see, and made the word of those who disbelieved the lowest, while the Word of Allah is the uppermost. And Allah is Mighty and Wise' (al-Tawbah 9: 40).

This hadith teaches us to be totally reliant upon Allah. Regardless of the type of hardship that we may face, strong reliance upon Allah will bring a way out for us. Allah says in the Qur'an: *'Whoever is conscious of Allah, He will make a way out for him... and whoever places his trust in Allah, He is sufficient for him'* (al-Talaq 65:3).

The Prophet Muhammad and Abu Bakr were in imminent danger, and a simple action from their enemies like looking under their feet, would have revealed them hiding in the cave. Abu Bakr, out of natural fear, said to the Prophet Muhammad that they could be caught and killed. However, the Prophet Muhammad reassured Abu Bakr that Allah is with them and no harm will come to them. Likewise, every Muslim should be reliant on Allah and know that no harm can be caused without the Will of Allah, and any harm that is caused, is only to test us in our response. It will be a test of our faith towards Him; the kind of test that makes us stronger. Afterall, without testing our reliance on Allah, how can we truly know how much love we have for Him in our hearts?

38

Striving to be Self-sufficient

عَنْ أَبِي سَعِيدٍ الْخُدْرِيِّ رَضِيَ اللهُ عَنْهُ أن رَسُولَ اللهِ صَلّى اللهُ عَلَيْهِ وَسَلّمَ قال وَمَنْ يَسْتَعْفِفْ يُعِفَّهُ اللهُ وَمَنْ يَسْتَغْنِ يُغْنِهِ اللهُ وَمَنْ يَتَصَبّرْ يُصَبِّرْهُ اللهُ وَمَا أُعْطِيَ أَحَدٌ عَطَاءً خَيْرًا وَأَوْسَعَ مِنَ الصّبْرِ

Abū Saʿīd ﵁ narrated that the Messenger of Allah ﷺ said: 'Whoever abstains from asking others, Allah will make him contented; whoever tries to make himself self-sufficient, Allah will make him self-sufficient; and whoever remains patient, Allah will make him patient. Nobody can be given a blessing better and greater than patience.'

The more our hearts are attached to Allah, the less we become in need of others and the more self-sufficient we feel. Similarly, the more we ask for things from others and rely upon them, the more we feel that we cannot do without them. There is no doubt that this would reduce the strength of our *tawakkul* (reliance upon Allah). Therefore, if we wish to have the quality of self-sufficiency and reliance upon Allah, we must practice it as regularly as possible, until eventually we find it becomes easy. In fact, it becomes second nature, just like any other thing which is practiced over and over again.

This hadith teaches us two things and these two things are underpinned by a third integral thing; patience. Begging is not a praiseworthy action and should be the absolute last resort. This hadith is not talking about those who are in abject poverty, but about those who are in hardship and have just about enough. For such a person, although life is a struggle, it is better to be patient and content with what they have, rather than asking others for money. When someone does this, they practice gratitude to Allah and most importantly, reliance on Allah. The fruit of this behaviour is that it develops one of the most important characteristics any person can have; the characteristic of *sabr* or patience. In this hadith, the Prophet Muhammad ﷺ tells us that patience is the greatest gift that a person can have. This is because patience is a quality that is needed in all situations. Patience ensures that we do and say the right thing at the right time and prevents us from transgressing. It is therefore no surprise that Allah has praised the patient ones in the Qur'an in so many different verses. *'Indeed, the patient ones will be given their reward without account'* (*al-Zumar* 39: 10).

Some people may think that they are naturally impatient and will always remain that way. This hadith shows us that patience is something that anybody can obtain if they work hard enough to practise it. We should constantly remind ourselves to be patient and avoid rushing into decisions, as well as ask Allah to grant us more patience. Over time, we will see the fruits of our efforts, and patience will become a natural quality within us.

39

If the Prophet ﷺ Did It, It's Good Enough for Me

عَنْ عُمَرَ رَضِىَ اللَّهُ عَنْهُ أَنَّهُ جَاءَ إِلَى الحَجَرِ الأَسْوَدِ فَقَبَّلَهُ فَقَالَ إِنِّى أَعْلَمُ أَنَّكَ حَجَرٌ لاَ تَضُرُّ وَلاَ تَنْفَعُ وَلَوْلاَ أَنِّى رَأَيْتُ النَّبِىَّ صَلَّى اللهُ عَلَيْهِ وَسَلَّمَ يُقَبِّلُكَ مَا قَبَّلْتُكَ

Umar ibn al-Khaṭṭāb narrated that he came near the Black Stone, kissed it and said: 'I know that you are just a stone and can neither benefit anyone nor harm anyone. Had I not seen the Prophet ﷺ kissing you, I would not have kissed you.'

Umar ibn al-Khaṭṭāb was the greatest Companion after Abu Bakr . He was one of the Companions whom we are explicitly commanded to follow due to his piety and great understanding of the religion. In this hadith, Umar teaches the Muslims two great lessons.

The first is that nothing can cause benefit or harm except Allah. Regardless of how sacred something is, it cannot bring about any harm or benefit. It is Allah alone who has the ability to cause harm and benefit, and they occur only with His permission. Despite this, we are still commanded to sanctify and honour those things that Allah has made sacred, such as the Kaaba and the Black Stone. Allah states in the Qur'an: *'And whoever honours the symbols of Allah - indeed, it is from the piety of hearts'* (*al-Ḥajj* 22: 32). This shows that even respect and love must be done with the right balance. Therefore, those who aggressively seek to kiss the Black Stone, even if this causes harm to them and others around them, have misunderstood the Sunnah. The Stone itself does not accept prayers. Allah accepts the prayers of a person wherever they are, and the one who tries to act upon the Sunnah of kissing the Black Stone during hajj or *'umrah*, but is unable to, due to the fear of potentially causing harm to other pilgrims, inconveniencing other worshippers, being inconsiderate or to avoid inappropriate contact with the opposite gender, shall not have their reward reduced in any way, and their prayers and supplications will still be accepted in the eyes of Allah.

The second thing that we are taught from the statement of Umar ؓ is that we should follow the Sunnah of the Prophet Muhammad ﷺ as much as we can. Sometimes we may not understand the wisdom behind a particular Sunnah, but we know that the Sunnah is revealed by Allah the Almighty, and so it can only be good for us. Therefore, the reward of the one who follows the Messenger of Allah ﷺ in all that he does, especially in his acts of worship, will be great; and we hope that following the Sunnah in this life will cause us to be with our beloved Prophet ﷺ in the next life.

40

The Reward of Spending Money on Family

عَنْ أَبِي مَسْعُودٍ عَنِ النَّبِيِّ ﷺ قَالَ إِذَا أَنْفَقَ الرَّجُلُ عَلَى أَهْلِهِ يَحْتَسِبُهَا فَهُوَ لَهُ صَدَقَةٌ

Abū Masʿūd ﷺ narrated: 'The Prophet ﷺ said: "If a man spends on his family (with the intention of having a reward from Allah) sincerely for Allah's sake then it is (rewarded as an act of) charity for him."'

Islam considers family values as a central pillar to creating a healthy society. It is important that every husband aspires to be the best husband and every wife aspires to be the best wife. They should strive to serve each other, care for each other and be patient with each other's shortcomings. No doubt, financial stress is a part of life. The vast majority of us will live a life wherein household finances will be a challenge or at least, an issue that needs attention. Creating a friendly home environment requires us to spend in order to meet the demands and needs of the family. Allah and His Messenger ﷺ wanted to reassure Muslims that spending money on their family is not in vain. Any money spent on the family is like giving money to charity. The virtue of charity is that it will not cause wealth to decrease, the money spent will be returned and the great spiritual reward (*thawāb*) of giving in charity will be achieved.

This hadith teaches us two important things:

Firstly, the importance of spending on the family, whether it is in the form of time or money. This means that there should be love and affection for everyone and the environment at home must be one of fun and joy. Sharing stories, jokes and playing games are good ways to help create this atmosphere.

Secondly, the hadith teaches us that Allah has created every opportunity in a Muslim's life to earn spiritual reward. Even though providing food, water, clothing, and all the basic necessities of the family is a legal obligation for the man, Allah has made it an opportunity for him to gain spiritual rewards as well. It is, therefore, mandatory that a person attempts to provide the best for his family, because his wealth will not decrease on account of it. Rather, Allah will return to him what he spends and reward him abundantly. Allah says in the Qur'an: *'Whatever wealth you spend in charity is to your own benefit for you spend merely to please Allah. So, whatever you spend in charity will be repaid to you in full and you shall not be wronged'* (*al-Baqarah* 2: 272).

It is worth mentioning that there are many women who participate in the maintenance of the family, whether by choice or due to circumstances. In such cases, women are also rewarded in like manner for helping provide for their family.